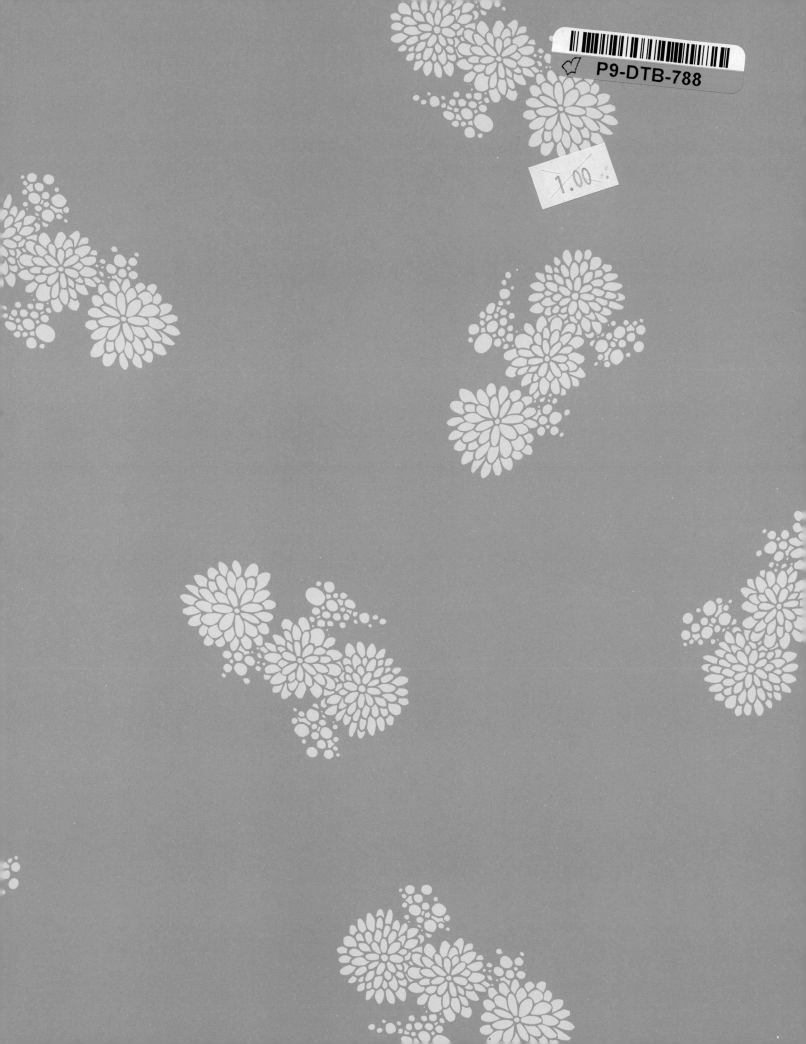

P9-DTB-788

1.00

a fine fleece

for max

a fine fleece

by lisa lloyd

knitting with handspun yarns

POTTER
CRAFT

NEW YORK

Copyright © 2008 by Lisa Lloyd
Photographs copyright © 2008 by Potter Craft

All rights reserved.

Published in the United States by Potter Craft, an imprint of the Crown Publishing Group,
a division of Random House, Inc., New York.
www.crownpublishing.com
www.pottercraft.com

POTTER CRAFT and CLARKSON N. POTTER are trademarks, and POTTER and
colophon are registered trademarks of Random House, Inc.

Thanks to the Craft Yarn Council of America (www.yarnstandards.com) for their
Standard Yarn Weight System Chart, which appears on page 155.

Library of Congress Cataloging-in-Publication Data

Lloyd, Lisa.
A fine fleece : 26 patterns for handspun yarn / By Lisa Lloyd.
          p. cm.
Includes index.
ISBN 978-0-307-34683-4
1. Hand spinning. 2. Spun yarns. I. Title.
TT847.L57 2008
746.1'2—dc22

                    2007028577

ISBN 978-0-307-34683-4

Printed in China

Design by Amy Sly
Photography by Alexandra Grablewski

10 9 8 7 6 5 4 3 2 1

First Edition

Photo opposite: Amanda cardigan, page 80.
Photo on page 2: St. Patrick sweater, page 108, with a ball of Jacob roving.

From left to right: Portland sweater, page 70; Fylingdales cardigan, page 40; October Frost cardigan, page 74; Gaelic Mist cardigan, page 130.

Four

Five

Foreword

Knitting with yarn that's been spun by hand is an exquisite experience. Every knitter knows how a handknit sweater differs from a store-bought one knit by machine. But the difference is twice as telling with garments we've knit from handspun yarn. They have an element of soul, an energetic charge, a liveliness that is impossible to replicate by machine.

Many handspinners—myself included—excel at producing small quantities of fiber. We buy an ounce from one farm, a few ounces from another farm, and we enjoy a few quiet hours of turning that jumbled fiber into orderly, even yarn. It's our morning paper, our nightly cup of tea, and we have basket upon basket of single skeins to show for it.

Occasionally we find a fiber that truly speaks to us. It comes alive in our hands, it almost spins itself. We don't want the adventure to end. The notion of spinning thousands of yards of yarn, of taking possibly weeks to do so, is not a burden. It is a delicious indulgence that we relish. These are the fibers we spin into sweaters.

As we spin these special fibers, our mind wanders. We process the day's events, we contemplate world peace, we dream of what this yarn will become, how the light will reflect against the fibers, how the stitches will feel on our needles, and how secure and beautiful we will feel when wrapped in the yarn's warmth.

We become intimately familiar with every ounce, every inch, every strand of fiber that passes through our fingers. We nurture it from furry mass to orderly openness to smooth strand to plump and eager skein. The rhythmic drafting, twisting, and releasing of our spinning breathes new life into these fibers as yarn. Before we even cast on that first stitch, we have already experienced what feels like a lifetime of pleasure.

That's just the beginning. Now we're faced with an even more difficult decision: What do we make with this special yarn? We look through magazines, books, and leaflets and hope for inspiration to strike. Sometimes it does, sometimes it doesn't. Sometimes we use our own design that turns into a blue-ribbon winner. But sometimes we remain stuck, unable to find a pattern that will really do the yarn justice.

Very few professional pattern collections exist for handspun yarns. Among those that do, the handspun is often added as an afterthought or shown only as the spark of inspiration from which a final garment—using millspun yarn—was created.

The book you are holding is a rare and welcome exception. It contains 26 patterns that were conceived from the very start for handspun yarns. The designs are fresh yet firmly rooted in classic knitting tradition, transcending what Lisa Lloyd calls "fashion's mercurial and dictatorial nature." Each pattern transitions seamlessly from handspun to millspun in pairings that Lisa rightly calls "fraternal twins." These are not reluctant commercial compromises, they are carefully chosen

Winding a skein of handspun Rambouillet crossbred and Mohair, for the October Frost cardigan, page 74, on a niddy noddy.

and entirely suitable alternative yarns that you can purchase instead of spinning yourself.

Why add millspun yarn options to a book of patterns for handspun yarns? First, because not all handspinners knit with handspun yarn all the time—and it would be a shame to limit these patterns to handspun alone. And second, because not all knitters know how to spin . . . at least not yet. I use the word "yet" both jokingly and seriously, because the path from knitter to spinner is, in many ways, inevitable.

I've seen even the mightiest millspun defender topple when faced with a roomful of handspinners at work. The mesmerizing sight of beautiful wheels in motion, of fine steady strands emerging from puffs of fiber, of the overall sense of calm fulfillment—it's too much. One day, some day, they all sit down and ask, "Can I try?"

Until that day, and well beyond it, this book will be a welcome companion.

—**Clara Parkes**
Editor and Publisher, KnittersReview.com

Introduction

The license plate on my car says simply "YARN." Someone once asked me if I was a knitter or a storyteller. I said a knitter, of course, but now I realize I do both. I tell a story with my yarn and my stitches, building one upon the other until, chapter upon chapter, the story is complete.

In the year of developing these projects, I revisited my creative past, embraced my creative future, worked through overwhelming grief, and entered a new decade of my life. Each step produced sweaters that waited patiently for their debut, to be marched out within these pages, all together, but with their separate personalities intact. The same designs, exhibited in both handspun and commercial yarns, appear as fraternal twins, not altogether that disparate but definitely not exactly alike. Taking skeins of yarn and turning them into pieces of knitting, each with a story, like a tiny microcosm of life itself, was a transforming experience for me.

Knitters and spinners alike will tell you how intensely personal their craft is—what it means to them to practice it—and they can mark important events in their lives by the sweaters they have knit or the yarn they have made.

Over the course of a year filled with personal changes, some poignant and bittersweet and some triumphant, this book was born. Some projects began their life as beautiful sheep fleeces that inspired a creative vision; some revealed themselves as the yarn itself wound its way around a bobbin in a blur of its very essence. Other yarns I sought out, reveling in the thrill of the hunt, in search of the perfect fiber to marry with my design.

For me, inspiration comes from all the facets of life, from colors and shapes found in nature to emotion—I attempt to display all of this in a three-dimensional, tactile form of color and fiber. It is difficult to put into words the feeling of placing a garment that represents so many things on one's body. My hope is that seeing the designs in different yarns and viewing how their demeanor changes, either with subtlety or deliberate contrast, will allow the knitter and the spinner to unlock the vision within and tell their own story with their knitting and spinning.

After more than thirty years of knitting everything from acrylic to buffalo, I know one thing: It's all about the yarn. And so my storytelling begins.

CHAPTER ONE

How to Use This Book

If you are a knitter with a passion for traditional knitting in wearable styles, then you're in the right place. If you are a spinner and love to design yarn, you will enjoy reading about how I design yarn from concept to finished product. I am continually amazed and inspired by knitters and spinners and how they make choices for their projects. This book will illustrate how a design can change not only by changing the color, but by changing the choice of fiber.

Every piece in this book is shown in both handspun and a commercially available yarn. In some cases the yarn choices are a deliberate contrast, and in others I spun a yarn to closely replicate a commercial equivalent. You will read about how I designed some of the handspun yarns used, whether the color or the fiber tells the story. Sometimes a certain fiber just fits the design without any real story behind it. Some stories also pertain to the choice of commercial yarn. Ultimately, I feel being a spinner has made me a better knitter simply by teaching me to see yarn differently. You don't need to spin to enjoy this book, but if you have even the slightest interest in learning to spin, I urge you to act on it.

Most knitters I know are fascinated with yarn and fiber and have well-established favorites, either in gauge, yarn company, or type. Being a spinner takes all these things to the next level and beyond. Handspinning opens up unlimited possibilities of yarn. If you can imagine a yarn, you can make it. As a knitwear designer, spinning has added a depth to my design work I never imagined possible. I love to play different fibers off each other, sometimes in unexpected ways, and design a garment specifically for that yarn. Non-spinners will learn a wealth of information from this book that can be utilized at the next visit to a yarn shop or sheep and wool festival, where handspun yarns are readily available for purchase. You will see yarn and fiber differently and have a new appreciation for what goes into the production of yarn, whether it's from a small antique mill or a large spinning facility.

The projects contained in *A Fine Fleece* range from scarves to sweaters and from simple textured stitch patterns to more complex cabled Arans. I'm usually hesitant to label my patterns with Skill Levels since what one knitter finds difficult may be easy for another. I always encourage knitters to continue to learn and grow at a comfortable pace. To help find your place, here is how I break down the Skill Levels required for the designs in this book:

INTERMEDIATE BEGINNER The knitter at this level should be comfortable with casting on, knitting and purling, and working back and forth and in the round on circular or double-pointed needles to make items such as scarves, hats, and sweaters without complicated shaping or complex stitch patterns. Also, a knitter at this level should have knowledge of basic increasing, decreasing, and finishing of a garment and be able to swatch and troubleshoot gauge problems.

INTERMEDIATE The knitter at this level should have completed several garments, including socks and sweaters with more complex shaping and/or finishing techniques, such as raglan or set-in sleeve shaping, edgings, and simple lace and cable patterns. An intermediate knitter should also be able to follow a chart.

EXPERIENCED The knitter at this level should be comfortable with nearly any pattern encountered, proficient in chart reading for multicable designs and lace, and comfortable with more complex shaping.

DESIGN THEORY

My design philosophy is simple: to create garments that transcend fashion's mercurial and dictatorial nature and suit any lifestyle. There is no reason that traditional garments can't work with a modern wardrobe. Classic design never goes out of style, and traditional knitting such as Arans, ganseys, and Shetland lace are essentially timeless. Natural fibers such as sheep's wool, alpaca, and mohair are also longstanding staples in fashion. Designs such as Espresso (page 58) and Le Smoking (page 84) are my interpretations of iconic fashion staples such as the Chanel jacket and the smoking jacket.

A WORD ABOUT SIZING

Most of my garments have basic shapes, and therefore fit a variety of bodies. In many patterns, I provide alternate body length options based on pattern motif lengths or whether I think something is more appropriate when knitting the sweater for a man or a woman. These small changes, such as the finished length and ease, can greatly affect how a sweater feels and looks. It can be difficult to make a garment truly unisex, and ease plays an important part. I give the finished chest measurement and the finished length from the shoulder for each sweater. These are the two most critical measurements in determining the desired fit of the garment. For garments that end just above the widest part of the hip, choose a finished size based on the actual chest measurement plus the desired ease. For example, for a 34" (86cm) actual chest, typically a 38" (96.5cm) or 40" (101.5cm) finished chest provides comfortable ease without being too boxy. If the hip is larger than the chest and the finished length falls below the hip, use the hip measurement plus the amount of ease that you want to determine the finished size. A great example of this is Portland (page 70). The Maine Organic version is shorter and closer fitting, perfect for trousers or a skirt and definitely more feminine in nature. The more masculine handspun version is longer and looser fitting, and the rich denim color makes it a perfect weekend sweater.

RULES TO KNIT BY

The first rule of knitting is there are no rules. Being a self-taught knitter and learning at a very young age has taught me to knit intuitively, not always by the book. With so many yarns available today, it can be difficult to make the right choice for the sweater you have chosen to knit. Be mindful of the suggested needle sizes and gauges on the yarn's label. These are suggestions only and are not carved in stone. Every knitter has his or her own knitting tension and many new knitters work rather tightly, loosening up over time. Come to think of it, I may have written a mistruth above. There is one rule: swatch. Swatch as if your life depended on it, because if you spend valuable time and money on yarn for a sweater

Photo on page 12: Handspun Karakul/Corriedale/Coopworth crossbred, for the Staghorn sweater, page 114.
Photo on page 10: Twilight scarves, page 64.

that doesn't fit . . . well, the fact that the sweater is bound to fit "someone" is simply not the point. Factor in the time you may have spent preparing the fiber and spinning it. Don't you want to be sure of the knitted outcome? I have been so sure a yarn will work for a certain project and swatched happily. While the gauge may have been spot on, the fiber wasn't appropriate because the color was too dark to properly show the pattern or the yarn was so dense the sweater would weigh five pounds when complete. Although a relatively small swatch can't tell you everything about the finished garment, it still tells you a lot. Take time to save time—*knit the swatch*.

FINISHING AND CARE OF YOUR KNITTING

Improper finishing of a garment can ruin beautiful knitting. Just as knitters have their favorite fibers, they also have their favorite finishing techniques. There is always something new to learn about edgings, selvedge stitches, or seaming. I like to allow for selvedge stitches in many of my patterns to make picking up stitches easier along a neck or button band edge or for tidy seaming.

I generally sew a garment together before washing and blocking. Sewing a garment together is usually necessary before knitting a neck edging on a pullover. If you sew the garment together before washing, all the yarn used in the project is washed at one time when the garment is complete. Some knitters prefer to block the individual pieces to size and then sew the pieces up. It is entirely your preference.

I wash all my woolens, from handspun skeins of yarn to finished sweaters, in Eucalan Woolwash (see Resources, page 153). It is extremely gentle and doesn't require rinsing. It does a thorough job of cleaning, and the remaining essential oils offer moth-repelling benefits. It softens yarn beautifully and makes fine fibers such as mohair and alpaca bloom into a lovely halo. My favorite method of washing skeins and sweaters is to fill a washing machine with enough warm water to cover the wool, and add a teaspoon of Eucalan Woolwash for each gallon of water estimated in the washer. Place the woolly items in the water and make sure they are completely submerged. Be sure that the machine is turned off and let the items soak for 20–30 minutes. Set the

washer to spin only, using the delicate cycle. Once the water has been spun out, lay the garment flat, either on towels or a blocking board, and gently pin to the final measurements. Alternatively, yarn and garments can also be soaked in a sinkful of warm water, but be careful not to handle the items too much while they are wet and soapy.

I don't recommend storing woolen items out of sight during the summer months. I keep all my woolens in my closet year-round, where I can keep my eye on them. They should be freshly cleaned at the end of the wearing season to prevent attracting moths or other pests. Never store wool items in direct sunlight or in extreme hot, cold, or damp conditions. It's also a good idea to go through and refold items periodically. When properly cared for, natural-fiber garments can give you many years of pleasure.

Remember that knitting is a journey, filled with stories and lessons learned along the way. Enjoying the process and being thankful for the opportunity to work with wonderful fibers will enhance your journey. A lifetime told with sweaters is a lifetime of joy, for you and anyone who shares your stories by wearing your sweaters.

CHAPTER TWO

The World of Handspinning

Thousands of years ago, we spun yarn out of necessity. Depending on the culture, fine threads of flax, silk, wool, or cotton were woven into fabrics that sailed ships, warmed shoulders, or covered cold beds in the winter. More than 5,000 years ago these threads were twisted either between the hands or on spindles, then much later on a variety of spinning wheels. A hair's breadth of time, just 500 years ago, brought the invention of the flyer and treadle wheel most commonly seen in use today. Later still, large mills produced yarn. Some antique spinning mills are still in existence. Regardless of the equipment used, spinning is nothing more than turning loose fiber into thread by means of inserting twist.

It has been said that spinning predates knitting, yet most of us probably learned to knit before taking up handspinning. In my case, because I had been knitting since I was six, learning to spin at the age of thirty-five was a far more academic process. Once I had the spinning basics down, I quickly developed procedures to reverse-engineer a yarn type. That's when the magic happened, and I realized I could truly design the yarn I desired.

All the handspun yarns in the following projects are basic two-ply yarns from roving that I purchased, had processed to my spec, or carded and blended myself on a drum carder. There are no complicated spinning techniques used, just the basic semiworsted spinning that most of us are initially taught. Instead, the design element I utilized is the use of color and texture in the yarn to tell a particular story. The yarns themselves are full of life and sometimes tell the story on their own without much in the way of stitch stories to enhance them. Other yarns are backdrops that allow more complicated stitch patterns or shaping to tell the story.

There are three basic concepts that I've illustrated with the designs. Some of these concepts overlap and spill over into subsequent chapters. Chapter Three: Light and Shadow portrays contrasts in several forms from the literal shadow play between knit and purl stitches to feminine versus masculine sweaters. The use of contrasting color and fiber alone can take a garment from town to country. Scale and perspective are explored in Chapter Four: The Forest and the Trees, where chunky yarn meets chunky cables and, sometimes, chunky cables express themselves in a more diminutive form. A higher-concept approach is taken in Chapter Five: Conceptual Stitches and Emotive Design, with sweaters that try to capture emotional essence and poetry. These sweaters have a more literal use of cables and stitches in the storytelling process.

Even though my personal design continuum has no set starting point, it does frequently begin with the fiber, so here is an overview of the fibers used for the projects in this book. This information will be useful in your own design process or in matching a yarn to a project.

WOOL

Nearly every project in this book contains sheep's wool. Sometimes the wool is enhanced by another animal fiber; sometimes it stands alone. A lifetime could be spent exploring wool as the sole source of spinning fiber. There are so many breeds of sheep worldwide that have so many different attributes that an entire encyclopedia could be written on sheep's wool alone. Regardless of the breed, all wool shares some basic characteristics. The most defining is its fineness, generally categorized by either the micron or Bradford count system. A micron, used predominantly in New Zealand and Australia and in the alpaca fiber industry worldwide, is a measurement of one-millionth of a meter. The lower the micron count, the finer the wool. Merino and subsequent breeds resulting from crossing merino sheep with other breeds are typically the finest wools available with micron counts ranging from 17–23. The other end of the spectrum is represented most notably in Ravensong (page 136), which is made with Cotswold wool that has an average micron count of 34–40. A system more commonly used in Great Britain and the United States, the Bradford count is a wool quality system to determine the fineness of wool. This old, established numbering system is based on how many 560-yard skeins of yarn could be spun from one pound of wool. The higher the number, the finer the wool, with Merino coming in at 80s and Cotswold running 36s–46s.

Even without this information, the fineness of most wool fleeces can be determined by the number of crimps per inch (2.5cm) in a lock or staple of wool. Crimp refers to the kinks or waves in each fiber—the more crimps per inch, the finer the fleece. Crimp is also useful in determining how best to spin and knit particular wool.

Since crimp refers to both the "hill and the valley," a knitter can quickly estimate the average needle size range suitable to a fleece by placing a knitting needle in the valley of a crimp and matching the size of the needle to the valley. For example, a very close and tight crimp in a fine merino would have a very small valley, hence a very small knitting needle would be most appropriate if this delicate wool were spun into a fine, small-gauge yarn. This is a very general guideline, but it does give a quick insight into how fine or bulky to spin the fleece.

Often a spinner can use crimp to predict the number of twists in a plied yarn. Fine wools can have 13 or more crimps per inch (2.5cm), and bulkier wools have 3–6 crimps per inch (2.5cm). The elasticity of wool and the resulting yarn is directly related to the amount of crimp along with the length of the staple. Finer wools such as merino are generally shorter stapled and softer, but pilling can occur when the ends of the fibers encounter abrasion. Long-stapled wools, like Border Leicester and some nonwool fibers, can lend a sheen and smoothness to yarn, but their length can mean a lack of elasticity. Most commercially spun yarns are not breed-specific, and the original crimp pattern is not apparent in the yarn's finished state. This can make it difficult to identify whether or not the knitted fabric will be elastic. However, because a length of yarn doesn't actually stretch when gently pulled doesn't mean that it won't knit into a soft and elastic sweater. Experience is the best tool in training your hands to recognize softer and "harder" wools.

The guidelines described above on crimp and the appropriate spinning and knitting methods should be viewed as starting points when buying and working with fleece and spinning fiber. There are exceptions to every rule, of course, and part of learning to spin and design yarn is playing with different wools and testing their boundaries. I particularly enjoy spinning fine lace yarn from coarser wools, and while I never expect them to be elastic or particularly soft, they make up for this with their exceptional character and tactile qualities.

Photo on page 16: Handspun singles on a drop spindle.

SHEEP BREEDS USED IN THIS BOOK

I was inspired to write this book early in my process of learning to spin, while I was still experimenting with different types of wool. Consequently, many of the garments here feature types and breeds of wool that are commonly available to a new spinner. I was also very fortunate to be introduced to some rare breeds of sheep as well, and many are featured in projects here. Below is a brief overview of the specific breeds used in this book. Most of the fibers come from spinners' small flocks, and many are crossbred with other breeds for various reasons such as color, staple length, and overall character of the wool. Being a designer, I naturally experimented with the blending of fiber and color for effect. Specifics about each fiber and how I arrived at the yarn that you see in each project accompany each pattern.

BLUE-FACED LEICESTER
Bradford Count: 56s–60s
Micron Count: 28–24
Staple Length: 3–6" (7.5–15cm)
The Leicester breeds are some of my favorites, with their long and curly locks and amazing shine. Blue-Faced Leicester is the finest of the lot, with a more delicate crimp pattern. I like to think of it as a more petite version of Border Leicester wool, but they both share the wonderful qualities of luster and soft halo when knitted. Blue-Faced Leicester is a treat to spin.

BORDER LEICESTER
Bradford Count: 36s–48s
Micron Count: 40–37
Staple Length: 6–8" (15–20.5cm)
Border Leicester is one of my favorite breeds to work with. With long and silky locks, the resulting yarn has a beautiful sheen and a soft halo. I consider it a bold wool with lots of personality. Espresso (page 58), knit in a gorgeous natural brown wool, uses a Border Leicester cross but exhibits the best qualities the breed has to offer a knitter.

CALIFORNIA RED
Bradford Count: 50s–54s
Micron Count: 31–28
Staple Length: 3–4" (7.5–10cm)
The California Red breed was developed in California in 1971 and is a wonderful and unusual fleece. The wool is a creamy color with auburn hairs interspersed throughout, giving it a slightly caramel appearance. Halcyon (page 102) shows how wonderful this effect can be with cabling. The crimp is fine, but the coarseness of the red hairs makes this a medium-fine fleece with good elasticity. California Red is a wool well worth seeking out and does not disappoint.

COOPWORTH
Bradford Count: 44s–48s
Micron Count: 39–35
Staple Length: 5–7" (12.5–18cm)
Coopworths were developed in New Zealand by crossing Border Leicester and Romney (page 20) sheep. A marriage made in heaven, the Coopworth fiber is strong with lustrous qualities and is very easy to spin and slightly coarser than Romney, making it great for heavier and highly textured sweaters.

CORMO
Bradford Count: 58s–64s
Micron Count: 23–21
Staple Length: 4–5" (10–12.5cm)
A relatively new breed introduced in the United States in 1976, the Cormo was developed in Tasmania in the early 1960s by crossing Corriedale rams with Merino ewes. It has a subtle sheen reminiscent of pearls, and while I love to spin a fine yarn from its silky locks, Narragansett Bay (page 94) is a fun experiment in spinning the same wool in three different weights. Cormo is a soft and elastic wool and suitable for next-to-the-skin wear.

CORRIEDALE
Bradford Count: 50s–58s
Micron Count: 33–26
Staple Length: 3–5" (7.5–12.5cm)
Another perennial favorite among spinners, Corriedale is a fine fleece that is widely available. The breed is itself the result of crossing longwool rams with Merino ewes, resulting in a relatively long and fine staple. This type of wool is very prevalent in commercially available spinning fiber as well. It appears here as a crossbreed with Coopworth in Rhinebeck (page 32); this mix is crossbred again with Black Welsh Mountain in Corduroy (page 36).

ICELANDIC
Bradford Count: Outer Coat: 50s–54s, Undercoat: 64s–70s
Micron Count: Outer Coat: 31–28, Undercoat: 22–19

Staple Length: Outer Coat: 4-10" (10-25.5cm),
   Undercoat: 2-3" (5-7.5cm)

Icelandic fleece is most familiar to knitters as the Lopi wool used in rustic winter sweaters. When the two coats are blended together, the resulting yarn has an amazing halo and can be quite soft if the outer coat (*tog*) is on the finer side. The short downy undercoat (*thel*) can be separated from the outer coat for fine lace spinning. Available in a wide variety of colors and patterns, Icelandic fleeces are highly coveted by spinners.

MERINO
Bradford Count: 60s–70s
Micron Count: 24–18
Staple Length: 2–4" (5–10cm)

Merino is considered by many to be the gold standard in wool. Merino is a beautifully fine-crimped wool, which can usually be worn directly next to the skin. Many breeders are developing flocks of gray and moorit (brown) sheep, and the Road Not Taken scarf (page 56) is an exceptional example of a lovely moorit fleece. Merino is perfect for fine spinning, making an elastic yarn with a matte finish.

RAMBOUILLET
Bradford Count: 60s–80s
Micron Count: 24–18
Staple Length: 2–4" (5–10cm)

Pure Rambouillet rivals Merino in fineness and softness and originated as a specific line of Merinos in France. Rambouillet appears here crossbred with other, less fine wools. When crossed with Romney (October Frost, page 74), it lends its elastic nature to a more medium wool, making a lofty yarn with a lovely finish.

ROMNEY
Bradford Count: 48s–54s
Micron Count: 35–40
Staple Length: 4–8" (10–20.5cm)

One of the most prevalent sheep breeds in North America, Romney wool comes in a variety of types and colors. It is one of the easiest to spin and is so versatile that one can never tire of it, in my humble opinion. There is Romney or Romney-cross wool in seven projects in this book, and no two share the exact characteristics. Romney breeders can focus on the type of crimp, from fine and delicate to more open and strong, or develop a flock of beautiful gray sheep by focusing on breeding for color. Romney is a perennial favorite among spinners because of its luster and the bouncy yarn that it makes.

SUFFOLK
Bradford Count: 56s–58s
Micron Count: 28–26
Staple Length: 2–3" (5–7.5cm)

A short-stapled wool that is highly durable and almost "old fashioned" begs to become cabled socks. The resulting design, Saxony, appears on page 90. Suffolk is a springy wool with a matte finish that can vary in softness.

RARE BREEDS

The American Livestock Breeds Conservancy (ALBC) classifies rare and endangered breeds of sheep as follows based on North American annual registrations:

CRITICAL estimated at fewer than 200 registrations

THREATENED estimated at fewer than 1,000 registrations

WATCH STATUS estimated at fewer than 2,500 registrations

RECOVERING Breeds that have exceeded the Watch Status but are still in need of monitoring.

BLACK WELSH MOUNTAIN
ALBC Status: Recovering
Bradford Count: 48s–56s
Micron Count: 33–26
Staple Length: 3–4" (7.5–10cm)

Although it doesn't appear here in purebred form, Black Welsh Mountain will always be close to my heart because it was one of the first wools that I spun by way of a crossbreed with Corriedale/Coopworth. The resulting sweater can be seen on page 36 (Corduroy). Black Welsh Mountain is a beautiful rich black-brown that ages gracefully, with the fleece gaining gray fibers as the sheep ages year by year. It is medium-luster wool, strong and durable and absolutely delightful to work with.

COTSWOLD
ALBC Status: Threatened
Bradford Count: 36s–46s
Micron Count: 40–34
Staple Length: 7–12" (18–30.5cm)

A luster longwool, the Cotswold locks are beautiful wavy ringlets that resemble the hair of the Angora goat. Extraordinary sheen and halo make this a wonderful and easy fiber to work with. Its ancient history gives it a moody allure that I tried to capture in Ravensong (page 136). The black and gray color of this particular fleece is somewhat unusual and singularly beautiful.

JACOB
ALBC Status: Threatened
Bradford Count: 48s–56s
Micron Count: 33–26
Staple Length: 3–6" (7.5–15cm)

Jacobs are very distinctive sheep with multiple horns. Jacobs have dark and light spots that can range from deep black-brown to auburn to lavender-gray. The fleece can be silky and lustrous or have a matte finish and a more crisp hand. The dark and light locks can sometimes differ in character from each other, and some spinners prefer to work with the two colors separately. The dark and light locks can be blended for a brown or gray heather, or striated for a variegated yarn. I am fortunate that my very first fleece was from a Jacob lamb, and the white portion is featured in the Town & Country Cardigan (page 46).

KARAKUL
ALBC Status: Threatened
Bradford Count: 50s and coarser
Micron Count: 29
Staple Length: 6–12" (15–30.5cm)

Karakul fleeces can sometimes be

The fiber from Barbara Parry's Border Leicester flock inspired the Twilight scarf, page 64.

double-coated, and they typically have no crimp. The wool is suitable for outerwear when it's on the softer side; otherwise, it is traditionally used for weaving. Staghorn (page 114) can attribute its woodsy character to the Karakul crossed with Corriedale/Coopworth.

NAVAJO-CHURRO
ALBC Status: Threatened
Bradford Count: Outer Coat: 36s and coarser, Undercoat: 62s
Micron Count: Outer Coat: 38, Undercoat: 22–23
Staple Length: Outer Coat: 4–14" (10–35.5cm), Undercoat: 2–4" (5–10cm)
Navajo-Churros are dual-coated and come in a wide variety of colors and patterns. Traditionally used in rug weaving, the durable wool can make lovely knitted outerwear. The outer hair portion of the fleece can be separated from the undercoat or blended together as it was for the Tilly scarf (page 88), for a rustic yarn.

SHETLAND
ALBC Status: Recovering
Bradford Count: 50s–60s
Micron Count: 30–23
Staple Length: 2–5" (5–12.5cm)
Shetland sheep are small, endearing, and full of personality. The fleece is available in a multitude of colors and textures sometimes with the more primitive dual coat made up of a longer and slightly coarser outer coat and a downy-soft undercoat. The more common single-coat fleece is quite fine and silky. Shetland wool is so lovely that I have chosen to feature it in a purebred state in Harriet (page 124).

EXOTIC FIBERS
MOHAIR (ANGORA GOAT)
Micron Count: 23 (First Shearing Kid) to 40 and coarser (Adult)
I considered naming this book *The Wool and Mohair Show*, given my propensity for adding mohair to nearly every project I design with handspun. Mohair simply cannot be beat for its visual interest, incredible halo and shine, and it takes dye like nothing else. While working with raw mohair can be challenging, it is well worth the extra time it takes to prepare the fiber for blending or spinning on its own. Mostly available in sparkling white, there are many breeders who specialize in naturally colored flocks that range from champagne (see the Twilight scarf, page 64) to inky black. Lacking natural elasticity, mohair spun on its own can be heavy and dense, and unless it's the first shearing (kid), it can be too scratchy to wear next to the skin. However, varying degrees of fineness can become design elements in yarns, and every project that contains mohair within these pages has distinct personalities.

ALPACA
Micron Count: 17–35
Running a close second for my favorite blending fiber is alpaca. Alpaca is a powerful design element, with its 22 natural colors and shimmering halo. The simple addition of alpaca to a yarn lends a mystique that everyone loves. Known for being hypoallergenic, many people who normally avoid other fuzzy fibers such as mohair and angora rabbit can wear alpaca. Alpaca fiber is shiny and slick and can have varying degrees of crimp. Unlike mohair, its fineness counteracts its lack of elasticity, and most alpaca yarns are lightweight if not springy. There are two types of alpaca: Huacaya is the most commonly available to spinners. It's used here in three projects in three different natural colors blended with wool. Huacaya, which is dense and crimpy, can generally have micron counts of 17–35 depending on the age of the animal. Suri is less common and has long, silky locks and similar micron counts.

LLAMA
Micron Count: 20–30
I often credit llama with being the fiber that enabled me to finally attain the "a-ha" moment in learning to spin—when it all seemed to come together for me. Generally not quite as fine or as slick as alpaca, the little handful of brushed llama was very easy for me to spin, and I've adored it ever since. Kearsarge (page 52) uses llama in a clever way for a warm and rustic sweater. When shopping for llama fiber, be aware that it can contain heavier guard hairs (a denser outer coat) along with the finer undercoat. I often enjoy the visual interest that guard hair brings to a project, but many people want the fine and smooth yarn of dehaired or very fine llama fiber. It is available in many beautiful natural colors and multicolored animals provide lots of spinning fun.

IT'S ALL
ABOUT YARN

As a handspinner, one of the biggest questions you will face is whether or not to process your own fiber. Many spinners choose to buy fiber that is already processed and ready to spin. This fiber can be dyed and blended with other fibers, or it can simply be naturally colored 100 percent wool. If you choose to process your own fiber from fleece to finished yarn, the possibilities are endless. This is a lot of work, some of it dirty, but if you're up to the task, it's well worth the time invested. I send some fleeces out for commercial processing, but more complicated blends, particularly color blending, I prefer to do myself on a drum carder. This way I can carefully control the final color or fiber blend to my satisfaction. I card and spin a sample to make sure I get the desired yarn and make adjustments as necessary.

Juxtaposition of fiber and pattern can create visual excitement when each element appears mediocre on its own. Many times I pair fibers to simply see what happens and then match them up to a knitwear design idea. Knitters will understand this concept as the traditional knitting stash, which spinners augment with skeins of handspun and roving waiting to be spun for a project down the road. I go about designing yarn using the same concepts that I apply to designing knitwear. Here are some of the basic concepts that I frequently employ when either designing a yarn or matching yarn to a particular project.

BLENDING WITH NATURAL COLORS

Wonderful and serendipitous handspun yarns can result from blending natural-colored fibers together. Amanda (page 80) and Two Hearts (page 148) both contain approximately 50 percent of the same charcoal gray Blue-Faced Leicester fleece. For Amanda I blended dark cinnamon alpaca with the Blue-Faced Leicester, and Two Hearts attributes its soft glow to pale fawn mohair. Neither resulting yarn is gray, and they differ greatly from each other simply because of the exotic fiber blend.

Wools like California Red allow me to showcase their unique properties and not worry about adding any additional fiber value to the finished yarn or project. It is easy, however, to become caught up in overengineering a yarn. Many yarn design "details" can become lost in the finished project or can even overwhelm the knitted design. When planning the California Red yarn for Halcyon (page 102), my original idea was to blend in some auburn mohair. While it would have been fun to match the tones of the mohair to the red hairs in the fleece, I realized that it was superfluous because the wool had so much color on its own. However, one could use auburn mohair with a white, more common, sheep's fleece to mimic the look of the California Red. Another example of successfully blending fibers is the purebred Jacob wool in Fylingdales (page 40), which resulted from a light gray and white Jacob fleece that I sent out for processing and requested to be well blended to the ethereal silvery color without any variegation.

Another way to blend fibers or colors with handspun is to ply two different singles (one "ply" of handspun) together. Kearsarge (page 52) uses a two-ply yarn that is one-ply wool and one-ply llama that happen to match nearly exactly in color. I use this technique when I want the best of two different fibers and their properties yet don't want to blend the fibers prior to spinning, or want the deliberate tweedy contrast if the two fibers are different colors. The Tilly scarf (page 88) uses gray and light brown Navajo-Churro wool plied together for a subtle tweed effect.

CRAFTING A COLOR STORY

Telling a story with color is a powerful experience in itself, and when texture is added, everything comes to life. It can take practice to learn how to dye fibers in multitonal colors and blend them together so they maintain some sense of identity and don't become muddy. It's also important to remember that once the fiber becomes yarn, the colors darken and some of the subtle tones can be lost in the twist. Again, spinning and knitting a sample is important to make sure your finished product is what you intended.

I take many of my color cues from nature and spend countless hours analyzing colors and textures and deciphering all the little bits that go unnoticed in the big picture. Portland (page 70) and Gaelic Mist (page 130) are good examples of how I chose one color and blended several shades together for a heathered effect. For St. Patrick (page 108), I wanted to design a more complicated color story. A conceptual Aran, it represents the rich culture of Ireland and Aran knitting. To make the yarn as rich as possible, I combined both texture and color interest by blending several colors of mohair with the green wool (itself a blend of two shades of green) to give a gemlike sparkle to the yarn.

MY METHODS FOR DYEING FIBER

There are several different methods for dyeing fiber and yarn that are described in wonderful books on the subject (Resources, page 153). I prefer to dye fiber prior to spinning unless I want a deliberately variegated yarn. Better still,

Photo opposite: Karakul/Corriedale/Coopworth crossbred roving (foreground) and Jacob roving (background).

I like to dye fleece prior to carding so I can achieve as smoothly blended colors as possible, which I prefer for textured knitting. As with any handcrafted product, subtle anomalies can occur, so it's best to alternate skeins of yarn when knitting with handspun to avoid unwanted striping.

When I'm designing a color and/or fiber-blend for a particular yarn, I take a very intuitive approach. Visualizing the final yarn or garment itself, I take apart the different elements and determine how much of each component contributes to the finished product. For example, using my knitting experience and commercial yarn knowledge, I estimate the percentage of mohair to put in a given yarn based on how much halo and shine I want the sweater to have. In the case of dyed or naturally colored mohair, I take into consideration the addition of the contrasting color. I love what I call *multidimensional colors*, where I dye fleece in several shades and card them together. When knitted, the heathered tones add incredible depth to the stitches in a way that simply dyeing the fleece with one shade of dye powder wouldn't achieve.

While I never tire of working with natural-colored animal fibers, planning and executing a complicated color story for a complex sweater design is an exhilarating experience. St. Patrick (page 108), Gaelic Mist (page 130), and Ruby (page 118) are the three most complex color stories here. St. Patrick is by far the most complex because the green wool is a careful blend of two shades of green and the mohair (approximately 25 percent of the finished yarn) is dyed in five different jewel tones. All the fiber was dyed in its clean-fleece state prior to carding, although I sometimes dye fleece while still greasy because the simmering dye pot cleans and dyes the wool at the same time. I always plan on losing about 30 percent of the gross weight of the fiber and add this amount to my estimated net weight. Then I determine the percentage by weight of each fiber to be blended, in this case 75 percent wool and 25 percent mohair. The wool is then divided up according to how many shades I'm dyeing, and this is where intuition comes into play.

When analyzing the colors of dye, I pick the main shade and then a coordinating lighter or darker shade for the heather effect that I'm looking for. Sometimes this could be in 50/50 proportions, but most of the time it's 75/25, 80/20, 70/30, or thereabouts. In the case of Gaelic Mist, several shades of green mohair are blended with the natural silver gray wool, and I didn't do too much planning ahead of time because I wanted to blend until it looked right. Dyeing extra fiber and carding samples ensures success and sometimes happy surprises can take the project in a new direction. Dyeing fiber in locks makes it very easy to meticulously blend while carding a small handful at a time. Each lock can take the dye differently, allowing a wider range of shades within the batch. I personally run into trouble when I dye roving and end up with spotty roving or an unwanted color. Re-dyeing roving is just asking for it to felt and become completely unspinnable.

The dyes I use are W. Cushing & Company and Prochemical & Dye (see Resources, page 153). They are very easy to use when following the manufacturer's directions for dyeing wool and other protein fibers. I prefer to dye small batches at a time because I'm working in my kitchen. Always keep track of the weight of fiber in each dye batch, exactly how much dye powder you use, and any other notes that will be helpful if you decide to repeat the batch at a later date.

BLENDING FIBERS BY DESIGN

It surprised me to discover that designing a fiber blend and creating the yarn is nearly as satisfying as designing knitwear. Being able to do both is the ultimate in total control of a project from beginning to end. Trinity (page 142) is the result of taking three of my very favorite fibers in similar natural shades, blending them in equal amounts, and designing a vest that continues the concept of *three*. The resulting yarn is deliciously rich in texture; however, it's not easy to pick out the three individual elements. For this concept, that wasn't important. The point was to marry the three fibers together synergistically to make the intended statement. Using fibers that are the same color and blending them together

leaves only the varying textures as clues to the fiber content. Conversely, St. Patrick's (page 108) multiple colors of mohair give themselves away, and the mohair really stands out from the wool. These are just two examples of the ways that you can blend fibers to either enhance a design or create the design itself. In many cases the yarn is the design and the garment form is secondary, or what I like to call a *canvas* for the fiber.

CARDING THE FIBER CANVAS

Unless I send fleeces out to be professionally processed into roving, my preferred method for fiber preparation is drum carding. The batts of fiber are in a neat package that makes it easy to spin, especially for the semiworsted method that I like to use. This is not to say I don't enjoy other blending methods, but for creating fiber in a "production" environment, drum carding can't be beat. While working on the projects for this book, I developed a carding and blending routine that served me well. The following is my method for color or multifiber blending.

I weigh out the different amounts of fiber to be carded based on the percentage of the total weight of finished batts that I need for the project. I card each component of the blend separately, whether it is different fibers or different shades of wool. These components get one pass through the carder, which makes a loosely formed batt that is not yet spinnable. My Duncan Fiber Enterprises carder (see Resources, page 153) makes approximately 2-ounce (56.7g) batts, and for the second pass, each component is divided up again, according to its percentage of the total in a 2-ounce (56.7g) batt. This yields batts that have consistent fiber content. At this point, I can simply card pieces of each batt together to randomly blend for even greater consistency. If anything needs further carding either to eliminate unwanted striping or for added spinning smoothness, I card until the texture is suitable. I find that dividing the carding process into these distinct steps creates a far more predictable product that can easily be repeated if necessary. Still, I always try to card a few extra ounces in case I find myself short of yardage in the spinning process.

SPINNING THE RIGHT YARN FOR THE JOB

All knitters know well the concept of gauge and how it affects the creation of the knitted fabric. We take these things for granted when shopping for yarn and can easily assess a commercial yarn by sight and touch and determine its appropriateness for our intended garment. This applies to spinning fiber as well, but it can sometimes be a challenge when looking at bags of raw fleeces and envisioning how they will transform from yarn to sweater. Obviously this takes lots of practice and experimentation. While I like to believe that one can spin anything they want from any fiber, some fiber still may not yield the fabric one had in mind.

A light and lofty wool such as Shetland or Romney can easily be spun into a variety of gauges and look great knitted up in nearly any pattern. But spinning an Aran-weight yarn out of 100 percent mohair is probably not the best idea. Blending mohair with a more appropriate wool will still provide the wonderful qualities of mohair, your Aran sweater won't weigh you down, and the cable stitches won't be obscured by fuzz. As a general rule,

less than 15 percent of an exotic or blending fiber will go unnoticed in the final yarn. I like to use a minimum of 20–25 percent of an exotic fiber added to wool for a subtle enhancing effect. The more exotic fiber that is added, the more its properties will contribute to the final knitted item. If the stitch pattern in the sweater stands out enough, and/or the stitch gauge is large enough, it can take more of a halo.

In many cases, fibers are blended according to "recipes" not just for color or texture but for their other properties, such as softness, elasticity, strength, or wearability. To add softness and bounce to the shine and glow from smooth, longer stapled wools like Leicester breeds, a springy wool with a similar staple length can be blended either in matching or contrasting tones. Maintain the overall yarn focus by using a higher percentage of the wool whose properties you want the most. Using ratios such as 80/20, 70/30, or 75/25 will give you the best of both worlds.

Sock yarn is a perfect example of using fiber for strength and wearability. I learned long ago that I much preferred knitting socks with yarn that contained nylon over mend-

ing socks that wore out too quickly. Commercial sock yarns typically contain 20 percent nylon fiber, so I copied this formula for my handspun yarn intended for socks. Nylon can also be dyed with the same dyes used for wool, so it can be easily matched and go virtually unnoticed to the eye, but the strength of the fiber is there for the longevity of the socks. Nylon is also a very soft fiber and can be added to fiber blends for softness along with durability. Nylon does not, however, make a yarn machine washable.

Most commercial yarns, unless they are labeled as breed specific, are a homogenous blend of wools chosen for their various properties, and may not even be from purebred animals. Large quantities of fleece purchased for this purpose are generally grouped by grade of fineness to maintain consistency from year to year. While there is nothing wrong with this method, the individual characteristics of a breed's wool is lost in the mix, and preserving these personalities is the highlight of buying and spinning breed-specific wool, even when it's crossbred.

All the handspun yarns used here are two-ply yarns. Some of the commercial yarns used are singles or one ply of yarn, which is usually formed by

the use of slim wisps of pencil roving lightly twisted together to give the finished yarn stability. Hand spinning a singles yarn can be challenging, because you want just the right amount of twist to hold the fibers together, yet not make them want to bias in one direction when knitted. If you choose to spin a singles yarn, it is best to use it in a pattern of knits and purls where the alternating stitches can counteract the yarn's natural tendency to slant in one direction.

One of the biggest challenges I faced when learning to spin was finding how much twist to insert into the singles and when plying the final yarn. Some of my early handspun yarn looks great in the skein but when knitted, it's far too hard and doesn't bloom at all. It can be very difficult to let go and literally let the single wind onto the bobbin, trusting that your finished yarn will be soft and wonderful to work with. Most handspun yarn also changes quite dramatically when the skeins are washed after spinning, and the yarn changes yet again when the finished garment is washed and blocked. I was amazed when the yarn in Rhinebeck (page 32), which was my very first handspun and represents quite a dramatic spectrum of twist

amounts, bloomed and blended together perfectly after washing the finished cardigan. It is barely noticeable that I alternated skeins of varying weights throughout the project. It was a very pleasant surprise for me, to say the least. Most commercial yarns also bloom and change when washed, which is another vital reason to swatch and wash the swatch as you would the finished garment.

A crucial part of my design process is to first allocate the tactile qualities of the knitted piece. Knits and purls at smaller gauges in the gansey knitting style need a wool that allows the stitches to pop. Traditionally these were "harder" wools with a smooth finish, but fine and soft wools such as Merino and Cormo do the job well. The tradeoff is that they are not as hard-wearing as something like Border Leicester. These are the compromises that need to be made frequently, yet they are also what make spinning so wonderful, being able to create a unique yarn exactly to your own specifications. Some knitters may believe that all wool is nearly the same—this is certainly far from the truth. If I had used something like Karakul or even Navajo-Churro for Le Smoking (page 84), the effect would

have been far different from the sensual and sexy jacket you see here, even though those wools would have provided infinitely interesting texture and halo as well.

PLAYING WITH GAUGE

Sometimes I use gauge as a design element if it's an appropriate use of the yarn. Some yarns work well in a multitude of gauges, so swatching with several needle sizes can be a useful experience. A fine example of this concept is Harriet (page 124). The DK yarn that would typically be worked at 5½ stitches to the inch (2.5cm) was worked at 4 stitches to the inch (2.5cm) instead. With the soft and forgiving nature of both the handspun and commercial yarns used, the resulting fabric is soft and drapey yet doesn't look loosely knit. This wouldn't work with just any yarn and would certainly not work with a harder worsted wool yarn. Using a looser gauge is perfect for the feminine lacey design of Harriet.

TECHNICAL SPINNING STUFF

Now that all the elements of handspun knitwear design are gathered together, it's time to get to the spinning itself. I thought knitting was a technical hobby until I embarked on handspinning. There is so much knowledge to soak up, and in the beginning it can be difficult to know what is relevant and what to utilize. Once you have mastered the basics of how to spin on a spindle or a wheel, the most crucial bits of information necessary to be successful are the amount of twist in the yarn, the thickness of the singles, and knowing how to measure both the singles and the finished yarn. Again, there are many great references on the technicalities of spinning and several are listed in the Resources on page 153.

I experimented with many of the measuring systems, and after many failed yarn attempts and hours of frustration, not to mention buying and selling several different spinning wheels, I finally came upon a fairly foolproof method that works for me. The most common method for measuring yarn is the wraps per inch (wpi) or wraps per centimeter. While this is a great way to initially get a feel for the thickness of various handknitting yarns,

it can be a very subjective measuring system as it is completely dependent on how tightly the yarn is wrapped around a ruler or wpi gauge. Using the wpi method, I would get close to the yarn thickness and knitting gauge I wanted, but it was invariably not *quite* right. Instead, I simply cut a sample of a commercial yarn in the weight I'm striving for and compare this to my handspun and keep checking it frequently to make sure I'm staying on track. Using a sample as a guide is also helpful when comparing the amount of twist in yarn and its overall feel. In the Resources, I list some information on wpi and twist amounts in yarns for a frame of reference.

TWIST

There is a direct correlation between the amount of twist and the amount of softness or hardness in the finished yarn. The tricky part is knowing how much twist a single needs and then how many twists per inch are necessary when plying those singles together. Because all the projects in this book use two-ply yarn, the discussion here will be limited to information relevant to spinning this type of yarn.

A singles yarn is never balanced because it only has twist energy going in one direction. Two singles spun the same way (usually clockwise) with the same amount of twist are then plied together and spun in the opposite direction. This act both adds twist to the plied yarn and subtracts some of the twist energy from the singles. Armed with that knowledge soon after learning to spin, I was overzealous, as I'm sure many new spinners are, when I first started designing yarn. I often ended up with yarn that was a little overtwisted, yet it didn't

kink up and look all that bad in the skein. So how do you know when enough twist is enough? The rule to keep in mind when plying a balanced two-ply yarn is the number of twists per inch in the two-ply yarn should be two-thirds of the twists per inch in the singles. Another handy fact is that you can also match the number of crimps in a sheep's fleece to the twists per inch in the finished yarn.

That mysterious thing called *ratio* and the whorls that come with a spinning wheel are simply the number of revolutions the drive wheel turns, and thus inserts twist into the singles with each treadle push and inch of fiber fed onto the bobbin. The difference between the diameter of the drive wheel and the diameter of the whorl is the ratio. The smaller the whorl, the higher the ratio, and the more twists per inch inserted into the yarn. I have three whorls with my wheel, and I like to think of them relative to the yarn weights that I spin with them. I use the smallest whorl for lace and fingering yarns, the middle for sport and DK, and the largest whorl for worsted and bulky yarns, as each whorl has two grooves (ratios) each. The different sized whorls make it easy when I sit down to spin a particular yarn. I can do so with minimal setup time, knowing my chosen whorl will be in the ballpark. It's still helpful to check every now and then to be sure the yarn has the right amount of twist. You can do this by pulling out a length of singles, doubling it back on itself, and counting the number of twists.

During the plying process, you can count the bumps in the yarn for the number of twists per inch. The more twists per inch, the harder or tighter the yarn will be. Conversely, less twists per inch yield a softer, fluffier yarn. Also, when you examine the plied yarn, the fibers should lay parallel along the length of the yarn. This is something that is easier to see with colored wool than white, and a magnifying glass can help with distinguishing the strands of fiber. It's also important that a plied yarn is balanced so the knitted fabric won't bias in one direction. Experience is the best teacher here, but for a quick check during plying, pull a length of yarn from the bobbin and let it droop down. It should hang straight and not twist back on itself. A finished skein of yarn should also hang straight, but usually there is a bit of a twist at one end, which generally disappears once the skein has been washed and the twist has been set.

All this technical data is great and useful when one is learning to spin and endeavoring to understand the basic principles. I really couldn't grasp all the subtleties of spinning without this knowledge. However, once you have spun a fair amount of yarn and spent some valuable time measuring twist, your eye becomes trained and soon you will be able to tell by sight and intuition if a yarn is right. Swatching a sample yarn is always a must, and I do it with every project.

PREPARING YARN FOR KNITTING

Always wash your handspun yarns to set the twist, remove any excess dirt or spinning oil, and prepare the skeins for knitting. I like to wash my handspun in Eucalan Woolwash, as I do with all my knitted items. If I feel a handspun yarn still has some sheep's grease, dirt, or spinning oil left in it, I'll wash it with either a mild dish soap or mild laundry detergent, making sure the yarn gets more than one soaking in plain water to remove any excess detergent, and sometimes adding a little Eucalan Woolwash to the final rinse bath to add back some softening lanolin. I gently soak the skeins using the same method as for washing finished woolens, spin them briefly or gently squeeze if washing in a sink, and hang the skeins to dry without weight.

I like to measure, catalog, and label each skein with its weight and yardage. This is the only way to be sure there is enough yarn for a project. It is also a great way to check the consistency of the spinning from skein to skein. I measure each skein's yardage and weigh it on a small scale with ⅛-ounce or 1-g increments, as in a food, baby, or postage scale. I then divide the yardage by the weight to determine the yards per ounce for that particular skein. Once I've done this for all the skeins in the project and have recorded the information on paper, I can clearly see any irregularities in the spinning. This, in a nutshell, is the concept of *grist*, which is simply the length per unit of weight in yarn. Grist is most commonly represented as yards per pound (ypp) or meters per kilogram. I like to use yards per ounce, because it's a finer measurement and more suitable to the smaller-sized skeins that handspinning produces. I do add up the total weight of all the skeins and the total yardage to determine the ypp as well. When choosing a skein for swatching, I figure out the average yards per ounce for all the skeins and choose a skein that is closest to this number. Use this skein for basing your average knitting gauge on a project. If there is much disparity between grist of the skeins, be sure to alternate thicker and thinner skeins every couple of rows to blend them together so that the difference is unnoticeable. It's also a good idea to record the wheel, ratio/whorl, and any other pertinent spinning information in case you want to replicate this yarn.

HOW MUCH FIBER PER PROJECT?

I'm often asked this question. The amount of fiber (ready to spin, not raw unwashed fiber) is completely dependent on how you intend to spin it. Knitters know intuitively that a bulky weight sweater, something that knits about 3½ stitches per inch, is most likely going to weigh more than a delicate Shetland sportweight cardigan worked at 6 or 7 stitches per inch. To help with your fiber buying, start compiling lists of some of your favorite commercial yarns and keep track of the yards or meters per skein and the skein's weight.

There aren't really any hard and fast commercial spinning standards, but there are some generalities regarding the amount of yardage per 50-gram, 3½-ounce, or 4-ounce skeins and specific knitting yarns. If you know your general yardages for various projects when buying commercial yarn, it's easy to convert that figure into the number of skeins, the size of those skeins, and finally the total weight of the project. That total weight is how much roving you should buy, allowing a few additional ounces for insurance. If you're shopping for raw fleece, remember you can lose 30 percent of the weight of the fleece or even more once the grease and dirt have been washed out.

This is also not the time to be frugal, because you will regret it later. Always buy extra fiber because you may go through a few ounces in the sampling process and you may change your mind about exactly what you're spinning and knitting. You can always trade extra fiber or yarn with friends. One of the most magical things about spinning fiber is that much of the time, it is a one-of-a-kind blend or fleece, and it is very difficult to match something later.

In closing, I want to remind you not to lose sight of how fortunate we are to have so many spinning choices. Some people choose to do all their spinning on hand spindles and never purchase a wheel. Some spinners are deeply committed to certain breeds of sheep or types of wool. And other spinners choose never to process their own fiber from raw fleece. Remember that whatever you choose to do, you are creating a unique and singular product that represents that unique and singular part of your own creativity. Use the information here as a springboard for your own journey into handspinning.

CHAPTER THREE

Light and Shadow: Studies in Contrasts

When I first began designing knitwear, I didn't always have a clear concept in mind for a particular garment; I simply sketched something in my head and began the design process without really thinking about what inspired it. After a while, it appeared to me that the design process was more fulfilling if I had a concept to work with, either as a literal and visual interpretation or a more high-concept execution such as conveying an emotional response in an abstract way. I also like to group garments to tell a more complex story, with the items within the group becoming the concept.

The garments in this chapter represent two different and basic contrasting ideas. The first is the marriage of traditional knitting with contemporary clothing. My first love is Aran and gansey knitting, with its rich heritage and endless surface design possibilities. This level of texture is a natural for tactile handspun yarns. I also love simple lace patterns, especially in the Shetland tradition. I'm charmed by little woolen bits filled with holes, like small windows when layered with pieces of heavily textured clothing.

CONTEMPORARY TRADITION

The first group of patterns, starting with Rhinebeck (page 32) and ending with Ancient Oak (page 44), illustrates how a traditionally inspired garment can change its demeanor based on ease and sizing and also the yarn and color used. Small adjustments to a design such as body length and other design details can greatly change the look and feel of a sweater and increase its personal expression. Creating the illusion of gender-specific garments simply by changing the yarn and color is also a powerful technique in knitwear.

TOWN & COUNTRY

The Town & Country group, starting with Town & Country (page 46), takes the contrasting ideas further, showing how the use of fiber can make a sweater either dressed up or dressed down. Again, these garments are very traditional in nature, but allow much room for personalization and exploring contrasting themes. In Chapters Four and Five I explore deeper concepts in designing knitwear, continuing the contrasting elements here.

rhinebeck

Rhinebeck is home to the New York Sheep and Wool Festival and is considered by many to be hand-spinning Mecca. I felt it was a fitting theme for the sweater knitted with my very first handspun yarn. As a new spinner, the yarn I made gradually became less chunky and more consistent. To blend all these skeins together, I alternated between thinner and thicker skeins throughout the garment to make a more homogenous fabric. I was very surprised at the wonderful result. I also wanted to be sure that the cardigan would clearly represent the wonderful contrasts of rustic handspun natural wool, a very old gansey stitch pattern, and a modern but timeless sweater design. This very simple and easy-to-knit cardigan fills that bill perfectly. The fiery red model, worked in Cascade 220 (see Resources, page 153), has a more modern feel.

Because I also wanted to turn tradition on its end as another way to explore contrasts, I chose to place the knit and purl stitch pattern on the lower portion of the sweater as opposed to the yoke area that is more in keeping with the fishing gansey tradition. The use of knit and purl stitches is a great example of knitting contrast. Knits and purls are integral to all knitting and are, in themselves, exact opposites of each other. This cardigan could be unisex, but to me it is the quintessential ladies' sweater that goes with anything and goes anywhere—especially to a sheep and wool festival or to the city for a day of shopping.

SKILL LEVEL ● ○ ○
Intermediate Beginner

FINISHED MEASUREMENTS
CHEST 39 (43, 46, 51)" (99 [109, 117, 129.5]cm)
LENGTH 22 (23½, 25, 26)" (56 [59.5, 63.5, 66]cm)

YARN (4️⃣) medium
1,400 (1,600, 1,700, 1,900) yds (1,280 [1,463, 1,555, 1,738]m) worsted weight
MODEL AT LEFT Handspun Corriedale/Coopworth crossbred (100%), natural gray

MODEL AT RIGHT 7 (8, 8, 9) skeins Cascade 220 Wool, 3½ oz (100g) skeins, each approximately 220 yds (201m), 100% Peruvian Highland wool, 2427 Red

NEEDLES & NOTIONS
US size 7 (4.5mm) circular needles, 29" (75cm) and 16–24" (40–60cm) long, or size needed to obtain gauge
One set US size 7 (4.5mm) double-pointed needles, or size needed to obtain gauge
Stitch holders
Stitch markers
Tapestry needle
5 buttons, ¾" (2cm) in diameter

GAUGE
20 stitches and 30 rows = 4" (10cm) in stockinette stitch. Adjust needle size as necessary to obtain correct gauge.

NOTE
The cardigan is worked in one piece, back and forth in rows, from the lower edge to the armhole. Back and Fronts are then worked separately and shoulders are joined with a three-needle bind-off. Sleeves are picked up around the armhole edge and worked downward in rounds to the cuffs.

left Handspun Corriedale/Coopworth crossbred right Cascade 220 Wool

rhinebeck

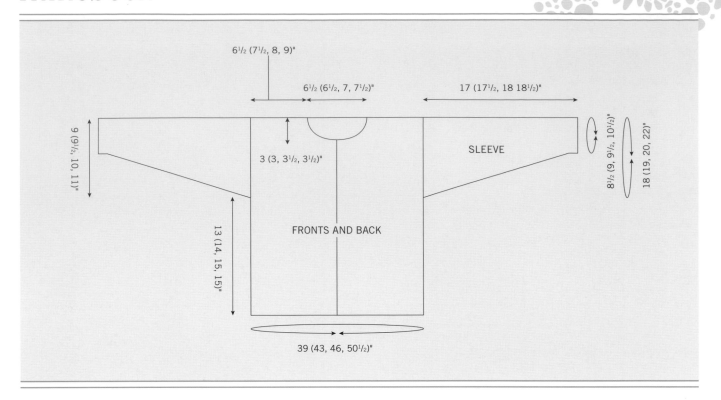

6½ (7½, 8, 9)"

6½ (6½, 7, 7½)"

17 (17½, 18 18½)"

9 (9½, 10, 11)"

3 (3, 3½, 3½)"

SLEEVE

8½ (9, 9½, 10½)"

18 (19, 20, 22)"

13 (14, 15, 15)"

FRONTS AND BACK

39 (43, 46, 50½)"

lower body

NOTE The first and last stitch of every row is worked in stockinette stitch for selvedge stitches at the front edges.

With the longest circular needle, cast on 192 (212, 232, 252) stitches. Do not join. Working back and forth in garter stitch (knit every row), work 48 (53, 58, 63) stitches for Right Front, place side marker, work 96 (106, 116, 126) stitches for Back, place side marker, work remaining 48 (53, 58, 63) stitches for Left Front. Continue in garter stitch for 8 rows (4 ridges on the right side), ending with a wrong-side row.

Begin Lower Body Pattern

ROW 1 Knit.

ROW 2 Purl.

ROW 3 K1 (selvedge stitch), *k2, p2; repeat from * to last the 3 stitches, k3.

ROW 4 P1, *p2, k2; repeat from * to last the 3 stitches, p3.

Continue working in Lower Body Pattern until the piece measures 13 (14, 15, 15)" (33 [35.5, 38, 38]cm) from the lower edge, ending with row 4 of Lower Body Pattern.

upper body

DIVIDE BACK AND FRONT FOR ARMHOLES

The Upper Body is worked in stockinette stitch. Work across 48 (53, 58, 63) stitches to marker for Right Front and place these stitches on a holder. Work across 96 (106, 116, 126) stitches for Back. Place remaining 48 (53, 58, 63) stitches on a holder for Left Front. Continue working in stockinette stitch on Back stitches until the Upper Back measures 9 (9½, 10, 11)" (23 [24, 25.5, 28]cm) from the armhole, ending with a wrong-side row. Place Upper Back stitches on a holder.

RIGHT FRONT

Place Right Front 48 (53, 58, 63) stitches on a needle, and beginning with the wrong side, work in stockinette stitch until Upper Front measures 6 (6½, 6½, 7½)" (15 [16.5, 16.5, 19]cm) from the armhole, ending with a wrong-side row.

SHAPE NECK

At the neck edge (beginning of right-side rows), bind off 5 (5, 6, 6) stitches, work to the end of the row. Bind off 2 stitches at the neck edge 2 (2, 3, 3) more times, then decrease 1 stitch at the neck edge every right-side row 7 (7, 6, 7) times as follows: K1 (selvedge stitch), ssk, work to the end of the row. Continue in stockinette stitch until Upper Front measures 9 (9½, 10, 11)" (23 [24, 25.5, 28]cm) or the same length as Upper Back, ending with a wrong-side row. Place remaining 32 (37, 40, 44) stitches on a holder.

LEFT FRONT

Place Left Front 48 (53, 58, 63) stitches on a needle, and beginning with the right side, work in stockinette stitch until Upper Front measures 6 (6½, 6½, 7½)" (15 [16.5, 16.5, 19]cm) from the armhole, ending with a right-side row.

SHAPE NECK

At the neck edge (beginning of wrong-side rows), bind off 5 (5, 6, 6) stitches, work to the end of the row. Bind off 2 stitches at the neck edge 2 (2, 3, 3) more times, then decrease 1 stitch at the neck edge every right-side row 7 (7, 6, 7) times as follows: Work across until 3 stitches remain, k2tog, k1 (selvedge stitch). Continue in stockinette stitch until Upper Front measures 9 (9½, 10, 11)" (23 [24, 25.5, 28]cm) or the same length as Upper Back, ending with a wrong-side row. Place remaining 32 (37, 40, 44) stitches on a holder.

JOIN SHOULDERS

Join the shoulders using a three-needle bind-off (page 152).

sleeves (MAKE 2)

With the 24" (60cm) circular needle and beginning at underarm, pick up and knit 90 (96, 100, 110) stitches evenly around the armhole. Place marker for the beginning of the round at center underarm and join. Sleeves are worked in stockinette stitch.

SHAPE SLEEVE

Decrease 1 stitch on each side of the marker every 4 rounds by working ssk at the beginning of the round and k2tog at the end of the round 16 (17, 18, 25) times, then every 6 rounds 8 (8, 8, 4) times. Change to the 16" (40cm) circular and double-pointed needles as necessary. Continue until the Sleeve measures 16 (16½, 17, 17½)" (40.5 [42, 43, 44.5]cm) from beginning. Work in garter stitch in the round (knit 1 round, purl 1 round) for 8 rounds (4 ridges). Bind off 42 (46, 48, 52) stitches purlwise.

finishing

LEFT FRONT BUTTON BAND

With right side facing, pick up and knit 108 (114, 126, 126) stitches along Left Front edge. Work in garter stitch for 7 rows. Bind off purlwise on right side.

RIGHT FRONT BUTTONHOLE BAND

Work same as for Left Front Band until 3 rows of garter stitch have been worked.

BUTTONHOLE ROW (RS): K23 (24, 24, 24) stitches, bind off 2 stitches, *k18 (19, 22, 22) stitches, bind off 2 stitches; repeat from * 4 times, knit to end.

NEXT ROW: Work across row, casting on 2 stitches over bound-off stitches. Work 2 more rows in garter stitch. Bind off purlwise on right side.

Cascade 220 wool

COLLAR

With right side facing, pick up and knit 84 (88, 98, 100) stitches evenly around neck edge. Working back and forth in garter stitch, slip the first stitch of every row and work until the collar measures 4" (10cm). Bind off purlwise on the right side of collar.

Weave in all loose ends and block gently. Sew buttons opposite buttonholes.

corduroy

Here I take a single gansey knitting element, the reverse stockinette stitch dividing ridge, and use it as the main design motif. Multiplying the ridges to replicate corduroy cloth, I placed the repeating pattern in the traditional position of the upper yoke and also played with the rhythm of the repeat of the ridges at the shoulders to mimic shoulder straps. The dark brown handspun version in Black Welsh Mountain crossbred wool is decidedly masculine, so to make a more feminine version, I added a ridged mock neck and used a soft and tweedy yarn.

SKILL LEVEL ○ ○ ○
Intermediate Beginner

FINISHED MEASUREMENTS
CHEST 40 (44, 48, 52)" (101.5 [112, 122, 132]cm)
LENGTH 25 (25½, 26½, 27)" (63.5 [65, 67.5, 68.5]cm)

YARN 🔒 light
1,550 (1,750, 1,900, 2,150) yds (1,418 [1,600, 1,738, 1,966]m) DK weight
SEATED MODEL Handspun Black Welsh Mountain/Corriedale/Coopworth crossbred (100%), natural dark brown
STANDING MODEL 8 (9, 10, 11) skeins Rowan Felted Tweed, 1¾ oz (50g) skeins, each approximately

192 yds (175m), 50% merino, 25% alpaca, 25% viscose/rayon, 152 Watery

NEEDLES & NOTIONS
US size 5 (3.75mm) circular needles, 29" (75cm) and 16–24" (40–60cm) long, or size needed to obtain gauge
One set US size 5 (3.75mm) double-pointed needles, or size needed to obtain gauge
Stitch holders
Stitch markers
Tapestry needle

GAUGE
22 stitches and 30 rows = 4" (10cm) in stockinette stitch. Adjust needle size as necessary to obtain correct gauge.

NOTE
The pullover is worked in one piece in the round to armhole. Back and Fronts are worked separately in rows and shoulders are joined with a three-needle bind-off. Sleeves are picked up around armhole edge and worked downward in rounds to the cuffs.

seated Handspun Black Welsh Mountain/Corriedale/Coopworth crossbred standing Rowan Felted Tweed

corduroy

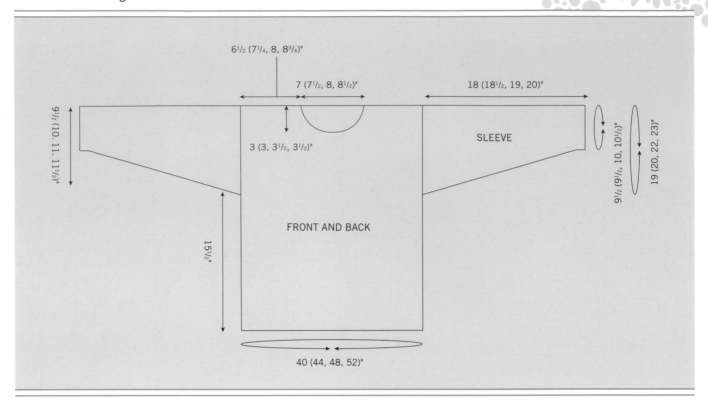

6½ (7¼, 8, 8¾)"

7 (7½, 8, 8½)"

18 (18½, 19, 20)"

9½ (10, 11, 11½)"

3 (3, 3½, 3½)"

SLEEVE

9½ (9½, 10, 10½)"

19 (20, 22, 23)"

FRONT AND BACK

15½"

40 (44, 48, 52)"

lower body

With longest circular needle, cast on 220 (242, 264, 286) stitches, join, being careful not to twist stitches, and place markers for beginning of round and after 110 (121, 132, 143) stitches for side "seams."
Work Welt Pattern
ROUNDS 1 AND 2 Purl.
ROUNDS 3 AND 4 Knit.
Repeat these 4 rounds for a total of 14 rounds, until there are 4 ridges, ending with round 2.
Lower Body Pattern
ROUNDS 1–10 Knit.
ROUNDS 11 AND 12 P18 (20, 22, 24) stitches, k74 (81, 88, 95) stitches, p36 (40, 44, 48) stitches, k74 (81, 88, 95) stitches, p18 (20, 22, 24) stitches.
Repeat these 12 rounds for pattern.
Continue working Lower Body Pattern until piece measures 15½" (39.5cm) from beginning, ending with round 10 of Lower Body Pattern.
NOTE Length can be adjusted here by working more or less repeats of the 12 rounds of pattern.

upper body

DIVIDE BACK AND FRONT FOR ARMHOLES

Working back and forth in rows and beginning with row 1, work across 110 (121, 132, 143) stitches for Upper Back. Place remaining 110 (121, 132, 143) stitches on a holder for Upper Front.

BACK
Upper Body Pattern
ROW 1 (RS) Purl.
ROW 2 (WS) Knit.
ROW 3 Knit.
ROW 4 Purl.
ROW 5 Knit.
ROW 6 Purl.
ROW 7 K18 (20, 22, 24) stitches, p74 (81, 88, 95) stitches, k18 (20, 22, 24) stitches.
ROW 8 P18 (20, 22, 24) stitches, k74 (81, 88, 95) stitches, p18 (20, 22, 24) stitches.
ROW 9 Knit.
ROW 10 Purl.
ROW 11 Knit.
ROW 12 Purl.
Continue to repeat the 12 rows of Upper Body Pattern until Upper Back measures 5¾ (6¼, 7¼, 7¾)" (14.5 [16, 18.5, 19.5]cm) from the armhole, ending with row 12 of Upper Body Pattern.

Work Welt Pattern

Work Rows 1–6 only of Upper Body Pattern until Upper Back measures 9½ (10, 11, 11½)" (24 [25.5, 28, 29]cm) from armhole, ending with row 5. Place all Back stitches on a holder.

FRONT

Place 110 (121, 132, 143) Front stitches on a needle. Beginning with row 1, work Upper Body Pattern until Upper Front measures 5¾ (6¼, 7¼, 7¾)" (14.5 [16, 18.5, 19.5]cm) from the armhole, ending with row 12.

Work Welt Pattern

Work rows 1–6 only of Upper Body Pattern, as for Back, until Upper Front measures 6½ (7, 7½, 8)" (16.5 [18, 19, 20.5]cm) from the armhole.

SHAPE NECK

Continuing with Upper Body Pattern as established, work across 45 (49, 55, 59) stitches, join a second ball of yarn, work across 20 (23, 22, 25) stitches and place these stitches on a holder for front neck, work to the end of the row. Working both sides at the same time, decrease 1 stitch at each neck edge every other row 9 (9, 11, 11) times as follows: Work across first shoulder until 3 stitches remain, k2tog, k1 (for neck selvedge). For second shoulder, k1 (for neck selvedge), ssk, work to end. Continue until Upper Front measures 9½ (10, 11, 11½)" (24 [25.5, 28, 29]cm) from the armhole—36 (40, 44, 48) stitches remain for each shoulder.

JOIN SHOULDERS

Join the shoulders using a three-needle bind-off (page 152).

sleeves (MAKE 2)

With the 24" (60cm) circular needle, pick up and knit 104 (110, 122, 126) stitches evenly around the armhole beginning at the underarm. Place marker and join. Sleeves are worked in rounds in stockinette stitch.

SHAPE SLEEVE

Decrease one stitch on each side of marker by working ssk at the beginning of the round and k2tog at the end of the round every 4 (4, 2, 2) rounds 20 (27, 4, 2) times, then every 6 (6, 4, 4) rounds 6 (2, 29, 32) times. Change to the 16" (40cm) circular or double-pointed needles as necessary. Continue until the sleeve measures 16½ (17, 17½, 18½)" (42 [43, 44.5, 47]cm) from the beginning—52 (52, 56, 58) stitches.

Cuff Welt

ROUNDS 1 AND 2 Purl.

ROUNDS 3 AND 4 Knit.

Repeat these 4 rounds 3 times, ending with round 4. Purl one round, then bind off purlwise.

Welt pattern in Rowan Felted Tweed

finishing

COLLAR

With the 24" (60cm) circular needle and right side of sweater facing, beginning at left shoulder seam, pick up and knit 94 (100, 108, 114) stitches evenly around neck edge, placing the held front neck and back neck stitches onto the left needle before knitting them. Knit 1 round.

Neck Edging

ROUNDS 1 AND 2 Purl.

ROUNDS 3 AND 4 Knit.

Repeat these 4 rounds three times, ending with round 4. For the optional mock turtleneck: Work these 4 rounds an additional 3 times. For both versions: Purl 1 round, then bind off purlwise.

Weave in all loose ends and block gently.

fylingdales

The Fylingdales cardigan is a more literal take on traditional gansey knitting. Based on the Robin Hood's Bay historic gansey pattern, this cardigan is another go-anywhere piece of clothing that will never go out of style. For the handspun version I chose a very old English sheep breed to lend a cozy feel and contrast with the Irish wool of the Black Water Abbey version. While I can't take credit for the wonderful juxtaposition of the rope cable and vertical bands of seed stitch, I revel in the symmetry of the combination and admire how it gives structure to the cardigan shape.

SKILL LEVEL ○○○
Intermediate

FINISHED MEASUREMENTS
CHEST 42 (45, 48, 51)" (106.5 [114.5, 122, 129.5]cm)
LENGTH 25½ (26, 26½, 27)" (65 [66, 67.5, 68.5]cm)

YARN medium
1,400 (1,600, 1,800, 2,000) yds (1,280 [1,463, 1,646, 1,829]m) heavy worsted weight
MODEL AT LEFT 7 (8, 8, 9) skeins Black Water Abbey Yarns Worsted Weight, 4 oz (113.5 g) skeins, each approximately 220 yds (201m), 100% wool, Ocean
MODEL AT RIGHT Handspun Jacob (100%), natural light gray

NEEDLES & NOTIONS
US size 5 (3.75mm) circular needles, 24" (60cm) long
US size 7 (4.5mm) circular needles, 24" (60cm) long, or size needed to obtain gauge
One set US size 5 (3.75mm) double-pointed needles
One set US size 7 (4.5mm) double-pointed needles, or size needed to obtain gauge
Cable needle
Stitch holders
Tapestry needle
5 buttons, ¾" (2cm) in diameter

GAUGE
16 stitches and 24 rows = 4" (10cm) in stockinette stitch using larger needles. Adjust needle size as necessary to obtain correct gauge.

WELT PATTERN
ROW 1 (RS) Purl.
ROW 2 (WS) Knit.
ROW 3 Knit.
ROW 4 Purl.
ROW 5 Purl.
ROW 6 Knit.
ROW 7 Knit.
ROW 8 Purl.

SEED STITCH
ROW 1 (K1, p1) across.
ALL OTHER ROWS: Knit the purl stitches and purl the knit stitches as they appear.

NOTE
The cardigan is worked in one piece, back and forth in rows, from the lower edge to the armholes. Back and Fronts are then worked separately and shoulders are joined with a three-needle bind-off. Sleeves are picked up around armhole edge and worked downward in rounds to the cuffs.

left Black Water Abbey Yarns Worsted right Handspun Jacob

fylingdales

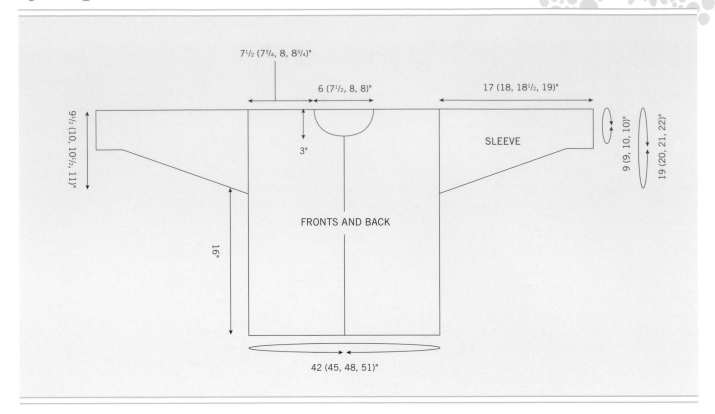

7½ (7¾, 8, 8¾)"

6 (7½, 8, 8)"

17 (18, 18½, 19)"

9½ (10, 10½, 11")

3"

SLEEVE

9 (9, 10, 10)"

19 (20, 21, 22)"

FRONTS AND BACK

16"

42 (45, 48, 51)"

body

NOTE The first and last stitch of every row is worked in stockinette stitch for selvedge stitch at front edges.

With the smaller circular needle, cast on 168 (180, 192, 204) stitches. Do not join.

ROW 1 (RS) K1 (selvedge stitch), (k2, p2) across to last 3 stitches, k2, k1 (selvedge stitch). Continue working in k2, p2 ribbing, keeping the edge stitches in stockinette stitch, until piece measures 3" (7.5cm), ending with a wrong-side row. Change to the larger needles and work in stockinette stitch for 5" (12.5cm), increasing 2 stitches evenly on the last wrong-side row, using the m1 increase—170 (182, 194, 206) stitches. Work Welt Pattern for 8 rows.

Body Pattern

ROW 1 (RS) K1, work 12-stitch repeat of Chart 3 times, p1, k1, work seed stitch over next 4 (6, 9, 12) stitches, place side marker for Right Front, work seed stitch over next 4 (2, 5, 8) stitches, work stitches 3–12 of 12-stitch repeat of Chart once, then work 12-stitch repeat of Chart 5 (6, 6, 6) times, p1, k1, work seed stitch over next 8 (6, 9, 12) stitches, place side marker for Back, work seed stitch over 4 (6, 9, 12) stitches, k1, p1, work stitches 9–12 of 12-stitch repeat of Chart once, then work 12-stitch repeat of Chart twice, work stitches 1–8 of 12-stitch repeat of Chart once, k1—43 (45, 48, 51) stitches for Right Front, 84 (92, 98, 104) stitches for Back, 43 (45, 48, 51) stitches for Left Front. Continue working in patterns as established until the piece measures 16" (40.5cm) from the beginning, ending with row 4 of Chart.

upper body

DIVIDE BACK AND FRONT FOR ARMHOLES

Work across 43 (45, 48, 51) stitches for Right Front and place on a holder. Work across 84 (92, 98, 104) stitches for Back. Place remaining 43 (45, 48, 51) stitches on a holder for Left Front.

BACK

NEXT ROW (WS) Working on Back stitches, increase one stitch at each edge purlwise for new selvedge stitches using the m1 method. Keep these stitches in stockinette stitch throughout. Continue in pattern as established on the Back stitches only until the armhole measures 7 (7½, 8, 8½)" (18 [19, 20.5, 21.5]cm), ending with row 4 of Chart. Repeat 8 rows of the Welt Pattern twice for a total of 16 rows. Place all stitches on a holder.

RIGHT FRONT

Place 43 (45, 48, 51) stitches from Right Front holder on the needle. Beginning with row 2 of Chart (wrong side), increase 1 stitch at beginning of the row purlwise using the m1 method (selvedge stitch for armhole edge)—44 (46, 49, 52) stitches. Work even in pattern as established, keeping the first and last stitches in stockinette stitch, until the armhole measures 6½ (7, 7½, 8)" (16.5 [18, 19, 20.5]cm), ending with a wrong-side row.

SHAPE RIGHT FRONT NECK

Bind off 8 (8, 9, 9) stitches at beginning of the next right-side row for the neck edge. Decrease 1 stitch at the neck edge every right-side row 6 (7, 7, 7) times as follows: K2tog on knit rows and p2tog on purl rows inside selvedge stitches to keep consistency with the Welt Pattern. *At the same time*, when the armhole measures 7 (7½, 8, 8½)" (18 [19, 20.5, 21.5]cm), ending with row 4 of Chart, work 8 rows of the Welt Pattern twice for a total of 16 rows. Place all stitches on a holder. Place remaining 30 (31, 33, 36) stitches on a holder.

LEFT FRONT

Place 43 (45, 48, 51) stitches from Left Front holder on the needle. Beginning with row 1 of Chart (right side), increase 1 stitch at beginning of the row knitwise, using the m1 method (selvedge stitch for armhole edge)—44 (46, 49, 52) stitches. Work even in pattern as established until the armhole measures 6½ (7, 7½, 8)" (16.5 [18, 19, 20.5]cm), ending with a right-side row.

SHAPE LEFT FRONT NECK

Bind off 8 (8, 9, 9) stitches at beginning of the next wrong-side row for the neck edge. Decrease 1 stitch at the neck edge every right-side row 6 (7, 7, 7) times as follows: K2tog on knit rows and p2tog on purl rows inside selvedge stitches to keep consistency with the Welt Pattern. *At the same time*, when the armhole measures 7 (7½, 8, 8½)" (18 [19, 20.5, 21.5]cm), ending with row 4 of Chart, work 8 rows of the Welt Pattern twice for a total of 16 rows. Place remaining 30 (31, 33, 36) stitches on a holder.

JOIN SHOULDERS

Join the shoulders using a three-needle bind-off (page 152).

sleeves (MAKE 2)

With the larger needle, pick up and knit 76 (80, 84, 88) stitches evenly around the armhole edge. Place marker and join. Working in stockinette stitch, shape Sleeves as follows: Decrease 1 stitch on each side of marker every other round by working ssk at the beginning of the round and k2tog at the end of the round 1 (0, 0, 3) time, then every fourth round 19 (22, 22, 21) times—36 (36, 40, 40) stitches remain. Work even until sleeve measures 14 (15, 15½, 16)" (35.5 [38, 39.5, 40.5]cm). Change to smaller double-pointed needles and work k2, p2 ribbing for 3" (7.5cm). Bind off loosely in pattern.

finishing

BUTTON BAND (Left Front for Women's; Right Front for Men's)

With the right side facing and the smaller circular needle, pick up and knit 110 (112, 114, 114) stitches along the front edge. Work in k2, p2 ribbing for 7 rows. Bind off loosely in pattern.

BUTTONHOLE BAND (Right Front for Women's; Left Front for Men's)

Work as for Button Band for 3 rows.
Make buttonholes: Work 2 (3, 2, 2) stitches, bind off 2 stitches, *work 24 (24, 25, 25) stitches, bind off 2 stitches; repeat from * 4 times, work to end. On the next row, cast on 2 stitches over the bound-off stitches. Work 2 more rows of ribbing, then bind off loosely in pattern.

COLLAR

With the right side facing and the smaller circular needle, pick up and knit 72 (72, 76, 80) stitches around the neck edge, omitting tops of button bands.

SET UP PATTERN (WS): K1 (selvedge stitch), (k2, p2) across to last 3 stitches, k2, k1 (selvedge stitch). Slip the first stitch of every row and work until the collar measures 4" (10cm), ending with the wrong side of the collar.

Work Welt Edging:

ROW 1 (RS OF COLLAR) Knit.
ROW 2 (WS) Knit.
ROW 3 Purl.
ROW 4 Purl.
ROW 5 Knit.
ROW 6 Knit.
ROW 7 Purl.
ROW 8 Bind off loosely knitwise on the wrong side.

Weave in all loose ends. Sew buttons opposite buttonholes. Block gently to measurements.

chart

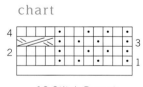

12-Stitch Repeat

key

☐ = K on RS, p on WS

• = P on RS, k on WS

⧄ = Slip 2 sts onto cn and hold in back, k2, k2 from cn

ancient oak

left Handspun Romney and Mohair with nylon **right** Wooly West Footpath Yarn

These lacy little socks use a simple Shetland feather lace motif that reminds me of oak leaves. For the light gray handspun socks, I designed a fiber blend with exceptional character and durability for hardwearing socks. Light gray Romney wool was blended with silver mohair in a 75:25 ratio. Then I blended this mix with nylon fiber so that nylon made up 25 percent of the total weight. I added the nylon for its durable properties. The soft and warm halo of the mohair is a more subtle contrast to the openness of the lace pattern. The spice-colored Footpath sock yarn represents the color of oak leaves in late autumn.

SKILL LEVEL ● ● ○
Intermediate

FINISHED MEASUREMENTS
Sized to Fit Women's Average Foot
Leg Length 7" (18cm)
Foot Length 10" (25.5cm)
Ankle Circumference 8½" (21.5cm)

YARN super fine
350 yds (320m) fingering weight
MODEL AT LEFT Handspun Romney and Mohair with nylon, natural light gray
MODEL AT RIGHT 2 skeins Wooly West Footpath Yarn, 2 oz (60g) skeins, each approximately 175 yds (160m), 85% wool, 15% nylon, Spice

NEEDLES & NOTIONS
One set of 5 US size 2 (2.75mm) double-pointed needles, or size needed to obtain gauge
Stitch markers
Tapestry needle

GAUGE
26 stitches = 4" (10cm) in stockinette stitch. Adjust needle size as necessary to obtain correct gauge.

cuff
Cast on 54 stitches loosely. Divide stitches evenly on 4 double-pointed needles as follows: 12 stitches, place marker, 18 stitches, place marker, 12 stitches, place marker, 12 stitches, place marker for the beginning of the round and the center of heel. Join, being careful not to twist stitches. Work k1, p2 ribbing for 1" (2.5cm).

leg
Begin Chart, working 6-stitch repeat around. Continue to repeat 20 rows of Chart until the leg measures 7" (18cm) from the beginning, ending with row 9.
NEXT ROW Working row 10 of Chart, work the first 41 stitches.

REARRANGE STITCHES FOR HEEL FLAP
Slip the remaining 13 stitches before the beginning of the round marker and the 14 stitches after the beginning of the round marker to the needle for Heel Flap—27 stitches. Leave remaining stitches unworked.

HEEL FLAP
Working on Heel Flap stitches only, turn and work back in stockinette stitch, increasing 1 stitch on the first row using the m1 method—28 stitches for Heel Flap.

ROW 1 Slip the first stitch knitwise, knit to end.
ROW 2 Slip the first stitch knitwise, purl to end.
Repeat these 2 rows until Heel Flap measures 2" (5cm).

TURN HEEL
ROW 1 (RS) K16, ssk, k1. Turn.
Slip the first stitch of every row purlwise.
ROW 2 Slip 1, p5, p2tog, p1. Turn.
ROW 3 Slip 1, k6, ssk, k1. Turn.
ROW 4 Slip 1, p7, p2tog, p1. Turn.
Continue in this manner, working to 1 stitch before previous slipped stitch, then work this stitch together with the next stitch until all stitches have been worked, ending with a wrong-side row.
With the same needle, work 8 stitches to the beginning of the round (center of Heel Flap), place marker.

HEEL GUSSET
With the free needle, knit the second half of the Heel Flap stitches. Continuing with the same needle, pick up 15 stitches along the right side of the heel—23 stitches on the needle, place second marker. Dividing stitches on the second and third needles, begin where indicated and work the 6-stitch repeat 4 times on next 27 stitches for instep, ending where indicated, place third marker. With another needle, pick up 15 stitches along the left side of the heel and knit across the remaining heel stitches—23 stitches on the last needle.

SHAPE GUSSET
NEXT ROUND Work to 3 stitches before the second marker, k2tog, k1, work 27 stitches of the instep as established, k1, ssk, work to end.
NEXT ROUND Work even.
Repeat these 2 rounds until 55 stitches remain. Knit two stitches together within the heel area on the last round—54 stitches remain.

foot
Continue working as established until the foot measures 8" (20.5cm) or 2" (5cm) less than the desired length. End at the beginning of the round marker.

SHAPE TOE
Work all toe stitches in stockinette stitch.
ROUND 1: Knit to 4 stitches before the second marker, k2tog, k2, ssk, work to 4 stitches before the third marker, k2tog, k2, ssk, work to end.
ROUND 2: Work even.
Repeat these 2 rounds until 30 stitches remain. Work round 1 only until 18 stitches remain.

finishing
Divide stitches evenly between 2 needles. Graft these stitches together using the Kitchener stitch (page 152).
Weave in ends.

chart

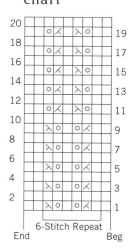

6-Stitch Repeat
End   Beg

key
☐ = K on RS, p on WS
⊠ = K2tog
⊠ = SSK
◻ = Yarn over (yo)

town & country

The Town & Country cardigan and pullover duo are classic examples of how a sweater can change expression with the choice of yarn, specifically with fiber and color. I set out to design the quintessential Aran sweater with all the hallmarks of what we recognize in Irish fisherman knits.

The daintiness of the cardigan is due to the exquisite blend of 50 percent Jacob lambswool and 50 percent alpaca. While cable knitting is generally better suited to smoother yarns, the softness of the alpaca halo gives a dreamlike quality to the stitches. The Jacob lamb fleece was my very first fleece purchase, and I carefully separated the white wool from the black to keep this sweater as white as possible. It still has the faintest tint of gray, as opposed to the creaminess of most white sheep's wool. I like to imagine an alternate countrified version of the cardigan, knit longer and oversized and in a more rustic wool, for a cozy sweater coat.

The denim blue pullover is a perfect weekend sweater for guys or girls. An easy-wearing classic wool such as Cascade 220 allows the cables to pop but is still very soft and comfortable to wear. Again, changing the length and the wearing ease of this pullover can greatly change the overall effect.

SKILL LEVEL ○ ○ ○
Experienced

FINISHED MEASUREMENTS
CHEST 38½ (42, 46½, 51)" (98 [106.5, 118, 129.5]cm)
LENGTH 22½ (22½, 26, 26)" (57 [57, 66, 66]cm)

NOTE
Length from the shoulder can be varied by 3½" (9cm) by working more or fewer repeats of the pattern charts (24 rows is approximately 3½" [9cm]). Please allow extra yardage for additional length.

YARN (4) medium
1,550 (1,650, 1,850, 2,050) yds (1,418 [1,509, 1,692, 1,875]m) worsted weight
CARDIGAN, LEFT Handspun Jacob (50%) and Alpaca (50%), natural white
PULLOVER, RIGHT 7 (8, 9, 10) skeins Cascade 220 Wool, 3½ oz (100g) skeins, each approximately 220 yds (201m), 100% Peruvian Highland wool, 4001 Blue

NEEDLES & NOTIONS
US size 5 (3.75mm) knitting needles
US size 7 (4.5mm) knitting needles, or size needed to obtain gauge
US size 5 (3.75mm) circular needles, 16" (40cm) long
Cable needle
Stitch markers
Tapestry needle
5 buttons for Cardigan, ¾" (2cm) in diameter

GAUGE
20 stitches and 28 rows = 4" (10cm) in moss stitch using larger needles. Adjust needle size as necessary to obtain correct gauge.

MOSS STITCH
ROW 1 (RS) (K1, p1) across.
ROWS 2 AND 4 (WS) Knit the knit stitches and purl the purl stitches as they appear.
ROW 3 (P1, k1) across.
Repeat these 4 rows for pattern.

left Handspun Jacob and Alpaca, 50/50 blend right Cascade 220 Wool

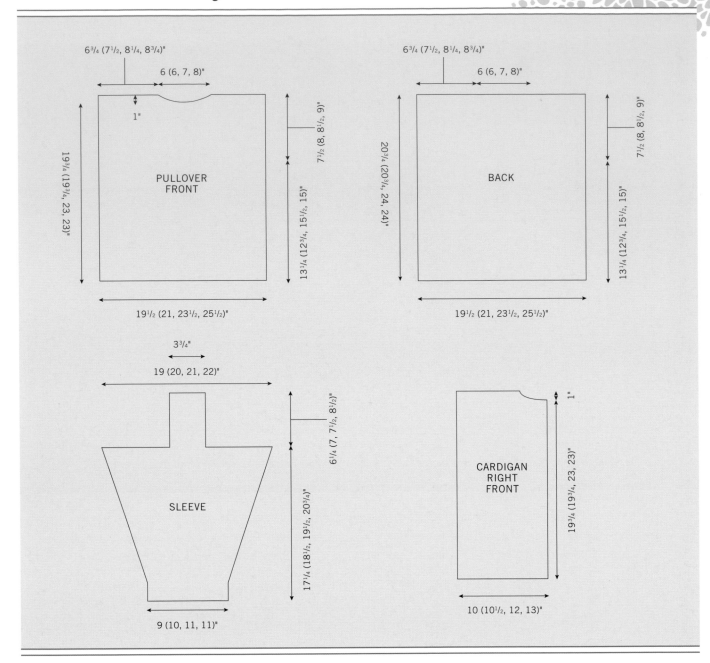

pullover back

NOTE One stitch at each edge is worked in stockinette stitch for selvedge stitch throughout.

With the smaller needles, cast on 124 (130, 142, 154) stitches.

RIBBING SETUP ROW K1 (selvedge stitch), p2, work 6-stitch repeat of Chart A across to the last stitch, k1 (selvedge stitch). Continue working Chart A until the ribbing measures 4" (10cm) in length, ending with row 4 of Chart A.

Work Dividing Ridge

ROWS 1 AND 3 K1, purl across to the last stitch, k1.

ROW 2 P1, knit across to the last stitch, p1.

ROW 4 Purl across, increasing 0 (1, 1, 1) stitch at each end of the row, using m1 left and m1 right methods, accordingly—124 (132, 144, 156) stitches.

Main Body Pattern

ROW 1 (RS) Change to larger needles. K1, work moss stitch over 10 (14, 20, 26) stitches, place marker (pm), work Chart B over 36 stitches, work Chart C over 30 stitches, work Chart D over 36 stitches, pm, work moss stitch over 10 (14, 20, 26) stitches, k1. Continue working all Charts until the piece measures 20¾ (20¾, 24, 24)" (52.5 [52.5, 61, 61]cm) from the beginning, ending with row 24 of Chart C. Bind off all stitches.

pullover front

Work same as for Pullover Back until the piece measures 19¾ (19¾, 23, 23)" (50 [50, 58.5, 58.5]cm) from the beginning, ending with row 16 of Chart C.

SHAPE FRONT NECK

Keeping continuity of charts, work across 44 (46, 51, 56) stitches for the left shoulder, join a second ball of yarn and work across center 36 (40, 42, 44) stitches and place on a holder for front neck, work across remaining 44 (46, 51, 56) stitches for the right shoulder. Working both sides at the same time, decrease one stitch at each neck edge every row 3 (2, 3, 5) times as follows: Work across first shoulder until 3 stitches remain, k2tog, k1 (for neck selvedge).

For second shoulder, k1 (for neck selvedge), ssk, work to end. Continue working remaining shoulder stitches until Front measures same as Back, ending with row 24 of Chart C. Bind off 41 (44, 48, 51) stitches for each shoulder.

sleeves (MAKE 2)

With the smaller needles, cast on 52 (58, 64, 64) stitches.

RIBBING SETUP ROW K1 (selvedge stitch), p2, work 6-stitch repeat of Chart A across to the last stitch, k1 (selvedge stitch). Continue working Chart A until ribbing measures 2" (5cm), ending with row 4 of Chart A.

Work Dividing Ridge

ROWS 1 AND 3 K1, purl across to the last stitch, k1.

ROW 2 P1, knit across to the last stitch, p1.

ROW 4 Purl across, increasing 8 (6, 4, 4) stitches evenly across row using the m1 method—60 (64, 68, 68) stitches.

Work Main Sleeve Pattern

ROW 1 (RS) Change to larger needles. K1, work moss stitch over 4 (6, 8, 8) stitches, pm, work Chart E over 50 stitches, pm, work moss stitch over 4 (6, 8, 8) stitches, k1 (selvedge stitch). Continue working Chart E, increasing one stitch at each edge (m1 inside selvedge stitch, working new stitches in moss stitch) every 4 rows 23 (19, 11, 17) times, then every 6 rows 1 (5, 13, 9) time—108 (112, 116, 120) stitches. Work even until Sleeve measures 17¼ (18½, 19½, 20¾)" (44 [47, 49.5, 52.5]cm) in length, ending with row 8 (16, 8, 16) of Chart E.

SHAPE SADDLE

Bind off 41 (43, 45, 47) stitches at the beginning of the next 2 rows—26 stitches. Continue to work the center 24 stitches of Chart E, keeping 1 stitch at each edge in stockinette stitch for selvedge stitch, until saddle measures 6¼ (7, 7½, 8½)" (16 [18, 19, 21.5]cm) in length, ending with row 8 or row 16 of Chart E. Bind off all stitches.

pullover finishing

Sew the long edges of saddles along shoulders of Front and Back. Sew the bound-off edges of Sleeves along the side edges of Front and Back. Sew side seams and sleeve seams.

NECKBAND

With the smaller circular needle and right side facing, pick up and knit 84 (90, 96, 102) stitches evenly around the neck edge beginning at the left side of Back, placing the held front neck stitches onto the other end of the circular needle before working them. Place marker for beginning of round and join.

Work Dividing Ridge

ROUNDS 1–3 Purl.

ROUND 4 Knit.

Work 6-stitch repeat of Chart A around for a total of 8 rounds. Bind off loosely in pattern.

Weave in all loose ends and block gently to measurements.

cardigan back

Work same as for Pullover Back.

right front

With the smaller needles, cast on 64 (64, 70, 76) stitches.

RIBBING SETUP ROW K1 (selvedge stitch), p2, work 6-stitch repeat of Chart A across to the last stitch, k1 (selvedge stitch). Continue working Chart A until the ribbing measures 4" (10cm) in length, ending with row 4 of Chart A.

Work Dividing Ridge

ROWS 1 AND 3 K1, purl across to the last stitch, k1.

ROW 2 P1, knit across to the last stitch, p1.

ROW 4 Purl across, increasing 0 (4, 4, 4) stitches evenly across the row using the m1 method—64 (68, 74, 80) stitches.

Work Main Body Pattern

ROW 1 (RS) Change to larger needles. K1, work Chart F over 16 stitches, work Chart D over 36 stitches, pm, work moss stitch over 10 (14, 20, 26) stitches, k1 (selvedge stitch). Continue working charts until the piece measures 19¾ (19¾, 23, 23)" (50 [50, 58.5, 58.5]cm) from the beginning, ending with row 16 (16, 16, 12) of Chart F.

SHAPE FRONT NECK

Keeping continuity of Charts, bind off 18 (20, 21, 20) stitches at the beginning of the right-side row, complete row, keeping the first stitch at the neck edge as a selvedge stitch. Decrease 1 stitch at the neck edge every row 3 (2, 3, 5) times as follows: K1 (selvedge), ssk, work to end. Work even until Front measures same as Back, ending with row 24 of Chart F. Bind off 43 (46, 50, 55) stitches for shoulder.

town & country

left front

Work ribbing and dividing ridge same as for Right Front.

Work Main Body Pattern

ROW 1 (RS) Change to larger needles. K1, work moss stitch over 10 (14, 20, 26) stitches, pm, work Chart B over 36 stitches, work Chart F over 16 stitches, k1 (selvedge stitch). Continue working charts until the piece measures 19¾ (19¾, 23, 23)" (50 [50, 58.5, 58.5]cm) from the beginning, ending with row 15 of Chart F.

SHAPE FRONT NECK

Keeping continuity of Charts, bind off 18 (20, 21, 20) stitches at beginning of the wrong-side row, complete row, keeping the first stitch at the neck edge as a selvedge stitch. Decrease 1 stitch at the neck edge every right-side row 3 (2, 3, 5) times as follows: Work across until 3 stitches remain, k2tog, k1 (selvedge). Work even until Front measures same as Back, ending with row 24 of Chart F. Bind off 43 (46, 50, 55) stitches for shoulder.

sleeves (MAKE 2)

Work same as for Pullover.

cardigan finishing

Sew the long edges of saddles along shoulders of Front and Back. Sew the bound-off edges of Sleeve along the side edges of Front and Back. Sew side seams and sleeve seams.

NECKBAND

With the smaller circular needle and the right side facing, pick up and knit 84 (90, 96, 102) stitches evenly around the neck edge, do not join. Work in moss stitch back and forth until the neckband measures approximately 1" (2.5cm). Bind off loosely in pattern.

BUTTON BAND (Left Front for Women, Right Front for Men)

With the smaller circular needle and the right side facing, pick up and knit 122 (122, 140, 140) stitches evenly along the front edge. Work in moss stitch for 7 rows, approximately 1" (2.5cm), then bind off loosely in pattern.

BUTTONHOLE BAND (Right Front for Women, Left Front for Men)

With the smaller circular needle and the right side facing, pick up and knit 122 (122, 140, 140) stitches evenly along the front edge. Work in moss stitch for 3 rows.

Handspun Jacob and Alpaca, 50/50 blend

BUTTONHOLE ROW FOR WOMEN Work 6 (6, 4, 4) stitches, bind off 2 stitches, * work 26 (26, 31, 31) stitches, bind off 2 stitches; repeat from * 3 more times, work last 2 stitches.

BUTTONHOLE ROW FOR MEN Work 2 stitches, bind off 2 stitches, * work 26 (26, 31, 31) stitches, bind off 2 stitches; repeat from * 3 more times, work last 6 (6, 4, 4) stitches.

FOR BOTH Next row: Work across row, casting on 2 stitches over bound-off stitches. Work 2 more rows of moss stitch, then bind off loosely in pattern.

Sew buttons opposite buttonholes. Weave in all loose ends. Hand wash and block gently to measurements.

chart a

6-Stitch Repeat

chart b

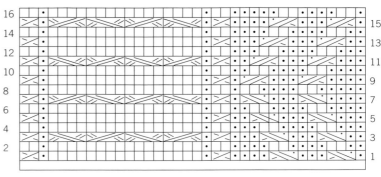

36 Stitches

chart c

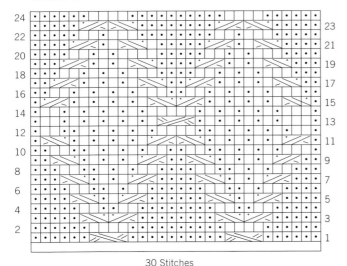

30 Stitches

chart d

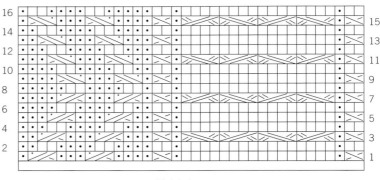

36 Stitches

chart e

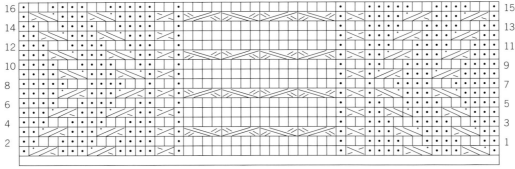

50 Stitches

chart f

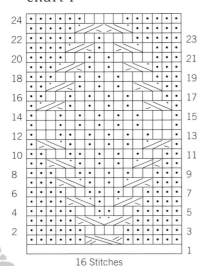

16 Stitches

key

☐ = K on RS, p on WS

• = P on RS, k on WS

= Slip next st onto cn and hold in back, k1, k1 from cn

= Slip next st onto cn and hold in front, k1, k1 from cn

= Slip next st onto cn and hold in back, k2, p1 from cn

= Slip 2 sts onto cn and hold in front, p1, k2 from cn

= Slip 2 sts onto cn and hold in back, k2, k2 from cn

= Slip 2 sts onto cn and hold in front, k2, k2 from cn

kearsarge

I must admit that Kearsarge may be my favorite design in this book. These two pieces are the ultimate in contrasts simply because of fiber choice. The concept for this pullover is intended to be pure country, whether that means spending the day in the woods or browsing antique shops. The mossy merino yarn can be worn next to the skin, while the llama and wool handspun version works well over a T-shirt or turtleneck. The contrasting stitch patterns work well together and add a lot of visual interest.

As a spinner, I learned to become very resourceful and make the most of limited amounts of fiber for projects. The wool and the llama fiber used in the yarn happened to match exactly. I wanted to have a yarn that was one ply of 100 percent wool and one ply of 100 percent llama but there wasn't enough llama for the entire project. There was, however, enough for the body of the sweater; the sleeves are knit with a two-ply yarn of 100 percent wool. To my mind, this small detail only enhances the overall charm of the sweater.

SKILL LEVEL ○○○
Intermediate Beginner

FINISHED MEASUREMENTS
CHEST 36 (38, 40, 42, 44, 46, 49)" (91 [96.5, 101.5, 106.5, 112, 117, 124.5]cm)
LENGTH 23 (24, 24, 25, 25, 26, 27)" (58.5 [61, 61, 63.5, 63.5, 66, 68.5]cm)

YARN (3) light
1,300 (1,400, 1,500, 1,650, 1,700, 1,800, 1,950) yds (1,189 [1,280, 1,372, 1,509, 1,555, 1,646, 1,783]m) DK weight
MODEL AT LEFT Handspun Blue-Faced Leicester/Border Leicester crossbred and Llama, two-ply yarn consisting of one ply 100% wool, one-ply 100% llama, natural light brown

MODEL AT RIGHT 8 (8, 9, 10, 10, 11, 11) skeins Jaeger Extra Fine Merino DK, 1¾ oz (50g) skeins, each approximately 137 yds (125m), 100% extra fine merino, 987 Cypress

NEEDLES & NOTIONS
US size 3 (3.25mm) knitting needles
US size 5 (3.75mm) knitting needles, or size needed to obtain gauge
US size 3 (3.25mm) circular needles, 16" or 24" (40cm or 60cm) long
Tapestry needle

GAUGE
22 stitches and 30 rows = 4" (10cm) in stockinette stitch and basketweave stitch using larger needles. Adjust needle size as necessary to obtain correct gauge.

SEED STITCH
ROW 1 (K1, p1) across.
ALL OTHER ROWS Knit the purl stitches and purl the knit stitches as they appear.

BASKETWEAVE STITCH
ROW 1 Knit.
ROW 2 Purl.
ROW 3 K2, *p4, k2; repeat from *.
ROW 4 P2, *k4, p2; repeat from *.
ROWS 5 AND 6 Repeat rows 3 and 4.
ROWS 7 AND 8 Repeat rows 1 and 2.
ROW 9 P3, *k2, p4; repeat from * to the last 5 stitches, k2, p3.
ROW 10 K3, *p2, k4; repeat from * to the last 5 stitches, p2, k3.
ROWS 11 AND 12 Repeat rows 9 and 10.

MISTAKE STITCH RIB
ALL ROWS *K2, p2; repeat from * to last 3 stitches, k2, p1.

left Handspun Blue-Faced Leicester/Border Leicester crossbred and Llama, two-ply yarn   right Jaeger Extra Fine Merino DK

kearsarge

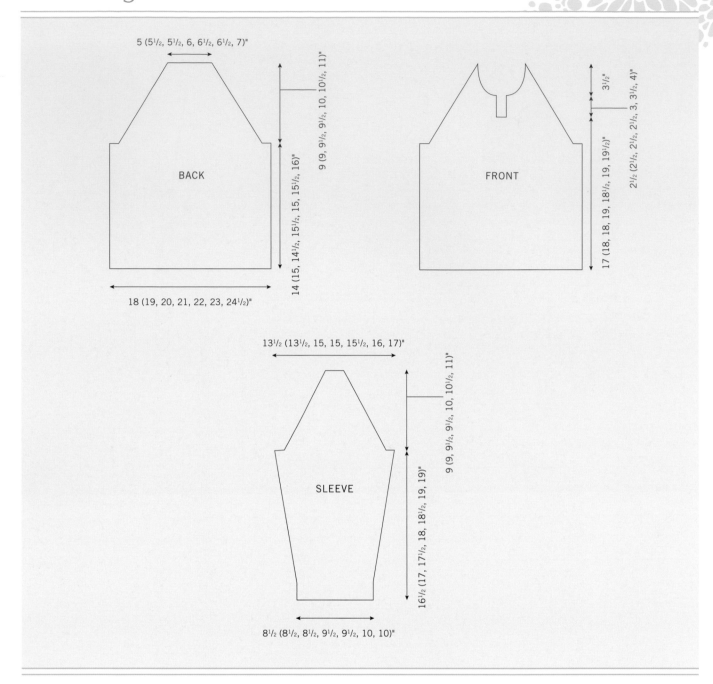

BACK

5 (5½, 5½, 6, 6½, 6½, 7)"

9 (9, 9½, 9½, 10, 10½, 11)"

14 (15, 14½, 15½, 15, 15½, 16)"

18 (19, 20, 21, 22, 23, 24½)"

FRONT

3½"

2½ (2½, 2½, 2½, 3, 3½, 4)"

17 (18, 18, 19, 18½, 19, 19½)"

SLEEVE

13½ (13½, 15, 15, 15½, 16, 17)"

9 (9, 9½, 10, 10, 10½, 11)"

16½ (17, 17½, 18, 18½, 19, 19)"

8½ (8½, 8½, 9½, 9½, 10, 10)"

back

With the smaller needles, cast on 88 (94, 100, 104, 110, 116, 122) stitches. Work in seed stitch for 1½" (4cm), increasing 10 (10, 10, 12, 12, 12, 12) stitches evenly across the last wrong-side row using the m1 method—98 (104, 110, 116, 122, 128, 134) stitches. Change to larger needles and work in stockinette stitch for 1½" (4cm). Beginning with row 1, work in basketweave stitch until Back measures 14 (15, 14½, 15½, 15, 15½, 16)" (35.5 [38, 37, 39.5, 38, 39.5, 40.5]cm) from the beginning, ending with a wrong-side row.

SHAPE ARMHOLE

Bind off 5 (11, 11, 11, 11, 11, 11) stitches at the beginning of the next two rows.

DECREASE ROW (RS) K1 (selvedge stitch), k2, ssk, work in basketweave stitch to the last 5 stitches, k2tog, k2, k1 (selvedge stitch).

NEXT ROW P4, work to the last 4 sts, p4.

Work Decrease Row every other row 27 (18, 23, 27, 27, 31, 33) times, then every fourth row 3 (8, 6, 4, 5, 4, 4) times—28 (30, 30, 32, 36, 36, 38) stitches. Back should measure 23 (24, 24, 25, 25, 26, 27)" (58.5 [61, 61, 63.5, 63.5, 66, 68.5]cm) from the beginning. Bind off remaining 28 (30, 30, 32, 36, 36, 38) stitches.

front

Work same as for Back, including armhole shaping, until Front measures 17 (18, 18, 19, 18½, 19, 19½)" (43 [45.5, 45.5, 48.5, 47, 48.5, 49.5]cm) from the beginning, ending with a wrong-side row.

SHAPE PLACKET

Keeping continuity of basketweave stitch and armhole shaping, work across to the center 6 stitches, join a second ball of yarn, and bind off the center 6 stitches, then work to the end of the row. Continue working both sides at same time with separate balls of yarn, keeping the edge stitches of placket in stockinette stitch for selvedge stitches, until Front measures 19½ (20½, 20½, 21½, 21½, 22½, 23½)" (49.5 [52, 52, 54.5, 54.5, 57, 59.5]cm) from the beginning, ending with a wrong-side row.

SHAPE NECK

Bind off 4 (4, 4, 4, 6, 6, 6) stitches at each neck edge once.
DECREASE ROW (RS) Left shoulder: work to last 3 stitches, k2tog, k1 (selvedge stitch). Right shoulder: K1 (selvedge stitch), ssk, work to end.
NEXT ROW (BOTH SHOULDERS) P2, work to last 2 sts, p2.
Work Decrease Row every other row 5 (6, 6, 7, 7, 7, 7) times.
Work until Front measures 23 (24, 24, 25, 25, 26, 27)" (58.5 [61, 61, 63.5, 63.5, 66, 68.5]cm) from the beginning, or same as Back. Bind off remaining 2 (2, 2, 2, 2, 3) stitches for each shoulder.

sleeves (MAKE 2)

With the smaller needles, cast on 47 (47, 47, 51, 51, 55, 55) stitches. Work in mistake stitch rib for 2" (5cm). Change to larger needles. Continue working mistake stitch rib, increasing 1 stitch at each edge by the m1 method every 6 rows 12 (10, 10, 10, 7, 4, 10) times, then every 10 (10, 8, 8, 8, 8, 8) rows 2 (4, 7, 6, 10, 13, 9) times, working new stitches into mistake stitch rib—75 (75, 81, 83, 85, 89, 93) stitches. Work even until Sleeve measures 16½ (17, 17½, 18, 18½, 19, 19)" (42 [43, 44.5, 45.5, 47, 48.5, 48.5]cm) from the beginning.

SHAPE SLEEVE CAP

Bind off 5 (11, 11, 11, 11, 11, 11) stitches at the beginning of the next 2 rows.
DECREASE ROW (RS) K1 (selvedge stitch), k2, ssk, work in mistake stitch rib to last 5 stitches, k2tog, k2, k1 (selvedge stitch).
NEXT ROW P4, work to last 4 sts, p4.
Work Decrease Row every other row 21 (9, 12, 14, 12, 15, 15) times, then every fourth row 6 (12, 12, 11, 13, 12, 13) times. Bind off remaining 11 (11, 11, 11, 13, 13, 15) stitches.

Jaeger Extra Fine Merino DK

finishing

Sew raglan seams. Sew sleeve and side seams.

PLACKET

With the smaller needles and right side facing, pick up and knit 16 (16, 16, 16, 18, 20, 22) stitches along the edge of the placket opening. Work in seed stitch for 1" (2.5cm). Bind off loosely in pattern. Repeat for the second placket edge. Overlap plackets and sew ends into place.

NECKBAND

With the smaller circular needle and the right side facing, pick up and knit 86 (90, 90, 92, 98, 98, 98) stitches evenly around the neck edge, beginning and ending at edges of plackets. Working back and forth, work in seed stitch for ½" (1.5cm). Bind off loosely in pattern.

Weave in all loose ends. Block gently to measurements.

road not taken

left Lorna's Laces Helen's Lace, 10-row repeat right Handspun Romney, hand dyed, 10-row repeat

I originally published this scarf pattern with the name Zigzag Lace Scarf. Not very imaginative for the conceptual nature of this book! When trying to come up with a more creative name, I started thinking about all the choices we face in our knitting and the roads we take along the way. I let my test knitter surprise me when she knit the merino handspun version with her choice of row repeat. She decided to use the full 20-row repeat, saying she was an overachiever. It was then that I realized that the zig-zag pattern represents the different directions and roads that we can take with knitting and spinning. I am always thinking of alternate versions of garments and wonder just how many different roads could be explored. Small projects such as this scarf allow unlimited possibilities. So many choices, so many roads to take.

Handspun Merino, natural moorit, 20-row repeat

SKILL LEVEL ●○○
Intermediate Beginner

FINISHED
MEASUREMENTS
Approximately 8" (20.5cm) x 60" (152.5cm) after blocking

YARN (1) super fine
400 yds (366m) lace or fingering weight
SCARF AT LEFT, OPPOSITE 1 skein Lorna's Laces Helen's Lace, 4 oz (114g) skeins, each approximately 1,250 yds (1,143m), 50% silk, 50% wool, Tuscany
SCARF AT RIGHT, OPPOSITE Handspun Romney (100%), hand dyed

SCARF AT RIGHT, THIS PAGE
Handspun Merino (100%), natural moorit

NEEDLES & NOTIONS
US size 6 (4mm) knitting needles, or size needed to obtain gauge
Tapestry needle

GAUGE
20 stitches = 4" (10cm) in Chart lace stitch. Adjust needle size as necessary to obtain correct gauge.

NOTE
Choose your own road by working all 20 rows of the chart, or just working rows 1–10 for main pattern.

Scarf

Cast on 38 stitches and work garter stitch (knit every row) for 4 rows.
NEXT ROW K2, beginning where indicated, work 12 stitches of Chart once, then work 11-stitch repeat of Chart twice more, k2. Continue working Chart, repeating either rows 1–20 or rows 1–10 and keeping the first 2 and the last 2 stitches in garter stitch, until scarf measures 60" (152cm) or desired length, stretching slightly, ending with a wrong-side row. Work garter stitch over all stitches for 4 rows. Bind off very loosely purlwise on the right side.

finishing

Weave in all loose ends. Hand wash and pin out carefully to finished measurements, allowing to dry completely before removing pins.

chart

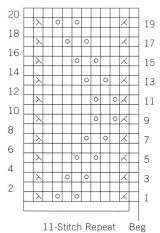

11-Stitch Repeat   Beg

key

☐ = K on RS, p on WS

⊿ = K2tog

⊠ = SSK

○ = Yarn over (yo)

espresso

Some sweater concepts are my homage to iconic fashion moments—in this case, the Chanel jacket. Since this cardigan is strictly feminine, I needed to explore contrasting imagery in other ways. Fiber and color will do that endlessly. The original model idea and the reason for the name stems from chocolate brown wool and the chic allure of a sidewalk café. The fiber I had intended to use for the project, a decadent blend of dark brown merino and alpaca, proved too dense in color for the subtle cable detail. The yarn also had a matte finish and, as lovely as it was, the lack of light reflection intensified the muddiness of the cable. The Border Leicester used here, however, has a shimmer that reflects light off the edges of the cables so even though you typically wouldn't knit a cabled sweater out of a yarn this dark, it works.

The alpaca blend yarn in the pink model also gives a sheen to the cables. Its super-girlie color harkens to the amazing tweedy boucle fabrics used in classic Chanel jackets. I tried to add my own little touches of detail with the back "vent" and the cabled cuffs and collar. The cardigan would be just as chic sans collar and worn with loads of pearls, of course.

SKILL LEVEL ● ● ○
Intermediate

FINISHED MEASUREMENTS
CHEST 38½ (40, 42½, 44, 46½, 48, 49½)" (98 [101.5, 108, 112, 118, 122, 125.5]cm)
LENGTH 21¼ (21¼, 22¼, 22¼, 23, 23, 23)" (54 [54, 56.5, 56.5, 58.5, 58.5, 58.5]cm)

YARN light
1,300 (1,400, 1,500, 1,600, 1,650, 1,750, 1,800) yds (1,189 [1,280, 1,372, 1,463, 1,509, 1,600, 1,646]m) DK weight

MODEL AT LEFT 6 (7, 7, 8, 8, 8, 8) skeins Nashua Creative Focus Worsted, 3½ oz (100g) skeins, each approximately 220 yds (201m), 75% wool, 25% alpaca, Carnation
MODEL AT RIGHT Handspun Border Leicester crossbred (100%), natural dark brown

NEEDLES & NOTIONS
US size 3 (3.25mm) knitting needles
US size 5 (3.75mm) knitting needles, or size needed to obtain gauge
US size 3 (3.25mm) circular needles, 24" (60cm) long

Cable needle
Stitch holders
Tapestry needle
7 buttons, ⅝" (1.6cm) in diameter

GAUGE
22 stitches and 28 rows = 4" (10cm) in stockinette stitch with larger needles. Adjust needle size as necessary to obtain correct gauge.

REVERSE STOCKINETTE STITCH
Purl all stitches on right-side rows and knit all stitches on wrong-side rows.

left Nashua Creative Focus Worsted right Handspun Border Leicester crossbred

espresso

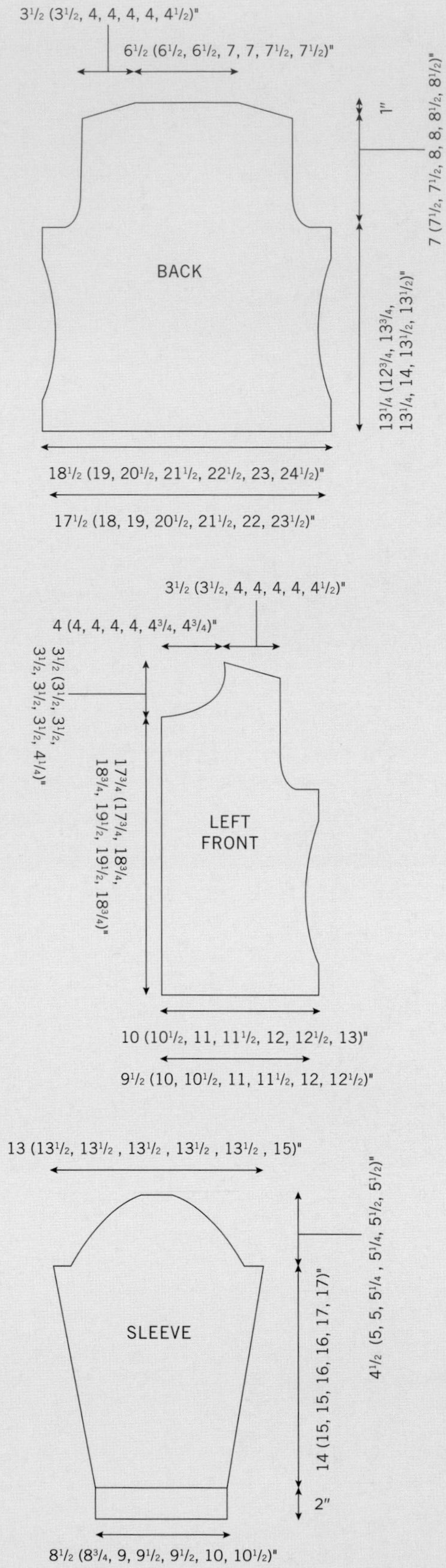

3½ (3½, 4, 4, 4, 4, 4½)"
6½ (6½, 6½, 7, 7, 7½, 7½)"
1"
7 (7½, 7½, 8, 8, 8½, 8½)"
BACK
13¼ (12¾, 13¾, 13¼, 14, 13½, 13½)"
18½ (19, 20½, 21½, 22½, 23, 24½)"
17½ (18, 19, 20½, 21½, 22, 23½)"
3½ (3½, 4, 4, 4, 4, 4½)"
4 (4, 4, 4, 4, 4¾, 4¾)"
3½ (3½, 3½, 3½, 3½, 3½, 4½)"
17¾ (17¾, 18¾, 18¾, 19½, 19½, 18¾)"
LEFT FRONT
10 (10½, 11, 11½, 12, 12½, 13)"
9½ (10, 10½, 11, 11½, 12, 12½)"
13 (13½, 13½, 13½, 13½, 13½, 15)"
4½ (5, 5, 5¼, 5¼, 5½, 5½)"
SLEEVE
14 (15, 15, 16, 16, 17, 17)"
2"
8½ (8¾, 9, 9½, 9½, 10, 10½)"

back

With smaller needles, cast on 89 (93, 99, 103, 109, 113, 119) stitches. Work 4 rows in garter stitch (2 ridges on the right side), ending with a wrong-side row. Knit 1 row, increasing 13 (13, 13, 15, 15, 15, 15) stitches evenly spaced across the row, using the m1 method—102 (106, 112, 118, 124, 128, 134) stitches. Purl 1 row. Change to larger needles and set up pattern as follows:

ROW 1 (RS) K1 (selvedge stitch), k42 (44, 47, 50, 53, 55, 58), work Chart A over center 16 stitches, k42 (44, 47, 50, 53, 55, 58), k1 (selvedge stitch).

Continue working as established for 13 rows.

SHAPE WAIST

DECREASE ROW (RS) K1 (selvedge stitch), ssk, knit across to the last 3 stitches, k2tog, k1 (selvedge stitch).

Continue to work Chart A for a total of 44 rows (approximately 6½" [16.5cm]), ending with row 4 of Chart A. Once these 44 rows are complete, work reverse stockinette stitch over the center 16 stitches for two rows.

At the same time, work Decrease Row every fourteenth row twice more—96 (100, 106, 112, 118, 122, 128) stitches. Work 13 rows.

INCREASE ROW (RS) K1 (selvedge stitch), m1 right, knit across the row until 1 stitch remains, m1 left, k1 (selvedge stitch)—98 (102, 108, 114, 120, 124, 130) stitches. Continue working Increase Row every fourteenth row twice more—102 (106, 112, 118, 124, 128, 134) stitches. Work until Back measures 13¼ (12¾, 13¾, 13¼, 14, 13½, 13½)" (33.5 [23.5, 35, 33.5, 35.5, 34.5, 34.5]cm) from the beginning, ending with a wrong-side row.

SHAPE ARMHOLE

Bind off 7 (8, 8, 9, 10, 10, 11) stitches at the beginning of the next 2 rows.

DECREASE ROW (RS) K1 (selvedge stitch), ssk, work across to the last 3 stitches, k2tog, k1 (selvedge stitch). Continue to work Decrease Row every other row 5 (6, 7, 8, 9, 9, 10) times more—76 (76, 80, 82, 84, 88, 90) stitches. Work even until the armhole measures 7 (7½, 7½, 8, 8, 8½, 8½)" (18 [19, 19, 20.5, 20.5, 21.5, 21.5]cm), ending with a wrong-side row.

SHAPE SHOULDERS

Using short rows (page 152), shape each shoulder at outside edge as follows:

ROWS 1 AND 2 Work to the last 7 (7, 8, 8, 8, 8, 8) stitches, wrap and turn.

ROWS 3 AND 4 Work to the last 13 (13, 14, 14, 15, 15, 16) stitches, wrap and turn.

ROW 5 Work across to the end of the row, picking up wraps.

ROW 6 Work across 20 (20, 22, 22, 23, 23, 24) stitches for shoulder and place them on a holder. Bind off 36 (36, 36, 38, 38, 42, 42) stitches for back neck. Work across remaining shoulder stitches, picking up wraps, then place them on a holder.

Back "vent" cable detail in Nashua Creative Focus Worsted

SHAPE ARMHOLE

Bind off 7 (8, 8, 9, 10, 10, 11) stitches at the beginning of the next right-side row. Work 1 row.

DECREASE ROW (RS) Knit 1 (selvedge stitch), ssk, work as established to end.

Work Decrease Row every right-side row 5 (6, 7, 8, 9, 9, 10) more times—42 (43, 45, 45, 46, 49, 50) stitches. Work even until the armhole measures 4½ (5, 5, 5½, 5½, 6, 5½)" (11.5 [12.5, 12.5, 14, 14, 15, 14]cm), ending with a right-side row.

SHAPE FRONT NECK

On the next wrong-side row, bind off 12 (13, 12, 12, 13, 16, 16) stitches.

DECREASE ROW (RS) Work across to the last 3 stitches, k2tog, k1 (selvedge stitch). Continue to work Decrease Row every right-side row 9 (9, 10, 10, 9, 9, 9) more times—20 (20, 22, 22, 23, 23, 24) stitches remain for shoulder. *At the same time*, when armhole measures 7 (7½, 7½, 8, 8, 8½, 8½)" (18 [19, 19, 20.5, 20.5, 21.5, 21.5]cm) and with a right-side row facing for the next row, shape shoulders.

SHAPE SHOULDER

Using short rows (page 152), shape shoulder at outside edge as follows:

ROWS 1, 3, AND 5 Knit across to the end of the row.
ROW 2 Work to the last 7 (7, 8, 8, 8, 8, 8) stitches, wrap and turn.
ROW 4 Work to the last 13 (13, 14, 14, 15, 15, 16) stitches, wrap and turn.
ROW 6 Work across all stitches, picking up wraps.
Place shoulder stitches on holder.

left front

With smaller needles, cast on 44 (46, 49, 51, 54, 56, 59) stitches. Work 4 rows in garter stitch (2 ridges on the right side), ending with a wrong-side row. Knit 1 row, increasing 11 (12, 12, 12, 12, 13, 13) stitches evenly spaced across row using the m1 method—55 (58, 61, 63, 66, 69, 72) stitches. Purl 1 row. Change to larger needles.

Set Up Pattern
ROW 1 (RS) K1 (selvedge stitch), k37 (40, 43, 45, 48, 51, 54), work Chart A over next 16 stitches, k1 (selvedge stitch).
Continue as established for 13 rows.

SHAPE WAIST

DECREASE ROW (RS) K1 (selvedge stitch), ssk, work as established across the row. Continue to work Decrease Row every fourteenth row twice more—52 (55, 58, 60, 63, 66, 69) stitches. Work 13 rows.
INCREASE ROW (RS) K1 (selvedge stitch), m1 right, work as established across row.
Work Increase Row every fourteenth row twice more—55 (58, 61, 63, 66, 69, 72) stitches.
Continue until Left Front measures 13¼ (12¾, 13¾, 13¼, 14, 13½, 13½)" (33.5 [23.5, 35, 33.5, 35.5, 34.5, 34.5]cm) from the beginning, ending with a wrong-side row.

right front

With smaller needle, cast on 44 (46, 49, 51, 54, 56, 59) stitches. Work 4 rows in garter stitch (2 ridges on right side), ending with a wrong-side row. Knit 1 row, increasing 11 (12, 12, 12, 12, 13, 13) stitches evenly spaced across row using the m1 method—55 (58, 61, 63, 66, 69, 72) stitches. Purl 1 row. Change to larger needles.

Set Up Pattern
ROW 1 (RS) K1 (selvedge stitch), work Chart B over next 16 stitches, k37 (40, 43, 45, 48, 51, 54), k1 (selvedge stitch).
Continue as established for 13 rows.

espresso

SHAPE WAIST

DECREASE ROW (RS) K1 (selvedge stitch), work as established to the last 3 stitches, k2tog, k1 (selvedge stitch).

Continue to work Decrease Row every fourteenth row twice more—52 (55, 58, 60, 63, 66, 69) stitches. Work 13 rows.

INCREASE ROW (RS) K1 (selvedge stitch), work across until 1 stitch remains, m1 left, k1 (selvedge stitch).

Work Increase Row every fourteenth row twice more—55 (58, 61, 63, 66, 69, 72) stitches.

Continue until Right Front measures 13¼ (12¾, 13¾, 13¼, 14, 13½, 13½)" (33.5 [23.5, 35, 33.5, 35.5, 34.5, 34.5]cm) from the beginning, ending with a right-side row.

SHAPE ARMHOLE

Bind off 7 (8, 9, 10, 10, 11) stitches at the beginning of the next wrong-side row.

DECREASE ROW (RS) Work as established to the last 3 stitches, k2tog, k1 (selvedge stitch). Work Decrease Row every right-side row 5 (6, 7, 8, 9, 9, 10) more times—42 (43, 45, 45, 46, 49, 50) stitches. Work even until the armhole measures 4½ (5, 5, 5½, 5½, 6, 5½)" (11.5 [12.5, 12.5, 14, 14, 15, 14]cm), ending with a wrong-side row.

SHAPE FRONT NECK

On the next right-side row, bind off 12 (13, 12, 12, 13, 16, 16) stitches.

DECREASE ROW (RS) K1 (selvedge stitch), ssk, work across row to the last st, k1 (selvedge stitch). Continue to work Decrease Row every right-side row 9 (9, 10, 10, 9, 9, 9) more times—20 (20, 22, 22, 23, 23, 24) stitches remain for shoulder. *At the same time*, when armhole measures 7 (7½, 7½, 8, 8, 8½, 8½)" (18 [19, 19, 20.5, 20.5, 21.5, 21.5]cm) and with a right-side row facing for the next row, shape shoulders.

SHAPE SHOULDER

Using short rows (page 152), shape shoulder at outside edge as follows:

ROW 1 Work to last 7 (7, 8, 8, 8, 8, 8) stitches, wrap and turn.

ROWS 2, 4, AND 6 Purl across to the end of the row.

ROW 3 Work to last 13 (13, 14, 14, 15, 15, 16) stitches, wrap and turn.

ROW 5 Work across all stitches, picking up wraps.

Place shoulder stitches on holder.

sleeve band (MAKE 2)

With smaller needles, cast on 18 stitches. Set up pattern as follows:

ROW 1 (RS) K1 (selvedge stitch), work Chart A over 16 stitches, k1 (selvedge stitch). Continue working chart until the band measures 8½ (8½, 9, 9½, 9½, 10, 10½)" (21.5 [21.5, 23, 24, 24, 25.5, 26.5]cm) in length. Bind off all stitches.

CUFF EDGING

With smaller needles and right side facing, pick up and knit 46 (48, 50, 52, 52, 56, 58) stitches along one side of Sleeve Band. Bind off on the wrong side purlwise. Repeat for second Sleeve Band.

sleeves (MAKE 2)

With larger needles, pick up and knit 46 (48, 50, 52, 52, 56, 58) stitches along the side of Sleeve Band. Work in reverse stockinette stitch for 3 rows. Change to stockinette stitch and increase 1 stitch at each edge of every fourth row 15 (19, 16, 22, 21, 21, 13) times, using m1 right and left accordingly inside the selvedge stitches and working the new stitches into stockinette stitch, then every sixth row 6 (4, 6, 2, 3, 3, 10) times—88 (94, 94, 100, 100, 104, 104) stitches. Work even until Sleeve measures 17 (17½, 17½, 17½, 18, 18, 18½)" (43 [44.5, 44.5, 44.5, 45.5, 45.5, 47]cm) from the beginning, ending with a wrong-side row.

SHAPE SLEEVE CAP

Bind off 7 (8, 8, 9, 10, 10, 11) stitches at the beginning of the next 2 rows.

Note Work decreases on right-side rows as follows: K1 (selvedge stitch), ssk, work across row as established to the last 3 stitches, k2tog, k1 (selvedge stitch).

Work decreases on wrong-side rows as follows: P1 (selvedge stitch), p2tog, work across row as established to last 3 stitches, p2tog through the back loops, p1 (selvedge stitch).

Decrease one stitch at each edge every other row 6 (7, 8, 9, 10, 10, 11) times.

Decrease one stitch at each edge of every row 18 (17, 17, 15, 13, 13, 11) times.

Decrease one stitch at each edge of every other row 0 (1, 0, 1, 1, 2, 2) times.

Bind off 3 (3, 3, 4, 4, 4, 4) stitches at the beginning of the next 4 rows.

Bind off remaining 14 (16, 16, 16, 16, 18, 18) stitches.

finishing

Join shoulders with a three-needle bind-off (page 152). Sew in Sleeves and sew side seams.

COLLAR

With smaller needle, cast on 32 stitches. Set up pattern as follows: K1 (selvedge stitch), work 8 stitches in stockinette stitch, work Chart C over 8 stitches, work 14 stitches in stockinette stitch. Continue as established until Collar measures approximately 16 (16, 16½, 16½, 16½, 18, 18½)" (40.5 [40.5, 42, 42, 42, 45.5, 47]cm) from the beginning, ending with row 4 of Chart C. Bind off all stitches.

Fold collar in half lengthwise with wrong sides together. Going through both layers of Collar, pick up and knit 14 stitches across each short end to close.

FOR THE CAST-ON EDGE Pick up with the wrong side facing and bind off on the right side in purl. Tack down the extra purl ridge neatly on the inside of the Collar, if desired.

FOR THE BIND-OFF EDGE Pick up with the right side facing and bind off on the wrong side in knit.

Sew Collar to the cardigan, being sure to catch both layers of Collar in the seam, with Collar edges meeting at the front edges of the cardigan.

FRONT BANDS

Button Band (Left Front)

With smaller circular needle and right side facing, pick up and knit 110 (110, 116, 116, 122, 122, 128) stitches evenly along the front edge, omitting the collar band. Knit three rows, then bind off loosely in purl on the right side.

Buttonhole Band (Right Front)

With smaller circular needle and right side facing, pick up and knit 110 (110, 116, 116, 122, 122, 128) stitches evenly along the front edge. Knit one row.

BUTTONHOLE ROW (RS) K8 stitches, *bind off 2 stitches, k14 (14, 15, 15, 16, 16, 17) stitches; repeat from * 5 times, bind off 2 stitches, k4.

NEXT ROW (WS) Knit across row, casting on 2 stitches over the bound-off stitches.

Bind off loosely in purl on the right side.

Sew buttons opposite buttonholes. Weave in all loose ends. Hand wash and block gently to measurements.

Collar detail in handspun Border Leicester crossbred

chart a

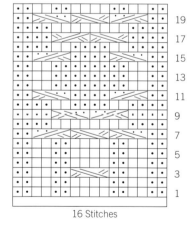

16 Stitches

chart b

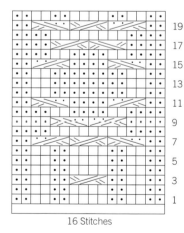

16 Stitches

chart c

3
1

8 Stitches

key

☐ = K on RS, p on WS

• = P on RS, k on WS

= Slip 2 sts onto cn and hold in back, k2, k2 from cn

= Slip 2 sts onto cn and hold in front, k2, k2 from cn

= Slip 2 sts onto cn and hold in back, k2, p2 from cn

= Slip 2 sts onto cn and hold in front, p2, k2 from cn

twilight

My friend Barbara Parry of Foxfire Fiber and Designs is a masterful fiber artist, and her use of color always inspires me. I also credit Barbara for cluing me into the magic of Angelina®. Angelina is a super-fine metallic fiber that can appear iridescent, holographic, metallic, or electric. The slightest sprinkle blended along with another fiber in the carding process can yield incredible luminosity and depth to a handspun yarn. A little of this fiber goes a long way, and experimentation is the best way to judge just how much Angelina you want in your finished yarn.

This sparkly lavender scarf features one of Barbara's colors, called Winter Sky, and made me think of twilight. There are times in late autumn and winter when the sky looks like a black-and-white photograph that has a hint of color and the stars beginning to twinkle. There are other times when the sky is an azure blue, a singular color here in New England that was captured with perfection by Maxfield Parrish, most notably in a painting called *Twilight*. The Zephyr laceweight scarf on page 66 is that exact azure color. The gray handspun version plays with the use of a contrasting yarn that is a different weight than the rest of the scarf, almost as if it were strung with pearls.

The transient nature of twilight throughout the seasons isn't unlike the ethereal beauty of hand-dyed yarn and spinning fiber. No two batches are ever alike, so taking advantage of the sheer perfection of a color blend at the moment it strikes your fancy is like capturing a moment of amazing colorwork painted by Mother Nature herself.

The larger version of Twilight illustrates how an interesting yarn can make a simple lace pattern very dramatic. The woodsy green and brown mohair laceweight from Lorna's Laces makes a very inviting wrap. This is an enchanting little lace pattern and perfect for playing with a multitude of yarns.

left Lorna's Laces Heaven right Handspun Border Leicester with trace amounts of Angelina®

left Handspun Corriedale and Mohair (contrast) right Jaggerspun Zephyr 218 Wool-Silk

twilight

SKILL LEVEL ○○○
Intermediate Beginner

FINISHED MEASUREMENTS
Scarf
Approximately 10 x 60" (25.5 x 152.5cm) after blocking
Stole
Approximately 22 x 65" (56 x 165cm) after blocking

SCARF YARN ⬛ super fine
400–600 yds (366–549m) laceweight to fingering weight
MODEL AT RIGHT, PAGE 65
Handspun Border Leicester (100%) with trace amounts of Angelina® from Foxfire Fiber and Designs in Winter Sky and Lupine (contrast)

MODEL AT RIGHT, OPPOSITE
1 cone Jaggerspun Zephyr 218 Wool-Silk, 1 lb (.45kg) cones, each approximately 5,040 yds (4609m), 50% merino wool, 50% Chinese tussah silk, Marine Blue
MODEL AT LEFT, OPPOSITE
Handspun Corriedale (100%) and Mohair (contrast, 100%), natural gray

STOLE YARN ⬛ super fine
600 yds (549m) laceweight to fingering weight
MODEL AT LEFT, PAGE 65 1 skein Lorna's Laces Heaven, 7 oz (199g) skeins, each approximately 975 yds (892m), 90% kid mohair, 10% nylon, Happy Valley

NEEDLES AND NOTIONS
SCARF
US size 5 (3.75mm) knitting needles, or size needed to obtain gauge
STOLE
US size 8 (5mm) knitting needles, or size needed to obtain gauge
Tapestry needle

GAUGE
FOR SCARF
20 stitches = 4" (10cm) in Chart Stitch using size US size 5 (3.75mm) knitting needles. Adjust needle size as necessary to obtain correct gauge.

FOR STOLE
16 stitches = 4" (10cm) in Chart Stitch using size US size 8 (5mm) knitting needles. Adjust needle size as necessary to obtain correct gauge.

NOTE
The garter ridge dividing the repeats of the lace can be worked in a contrasting yarn, by way of a contrast color or even in a contrasting weight, as shown in the handspun scarf version here. The choice of yarns greatly affects gauge with this pattern. Swatch to get a feel for how open you want your Twilight lace to appear.

scarf

Note For a two-color scarf or stole, work all garter rows, eyelet rows, and rows 11–14 of chart with a contrast yarn.

Cast on 46 stitches and knit 4 rows (2 garter ridges on the right side).

EYELET ROW (RS) K2, *yo, k2tog; repeat from * to the last 2 stitches, k2. Work 4 rows in garter stitch, increasing one stitch on the last row—47 stitches.

Set Up Twilight Chart
ROW 1 (RS) K2, work 15 stitches of Chart once, then repeat the 14-stitch repeat twice, k2. Continue in this manner, keeping first 2 and last 2 stitches in garter stitch, until Scarf measures approximately 59" (150cm) or 1" (2.5cm) less than desired length, stretching slightly, ending with row 12 of Chart and decreasing 1 stitch by k2tog anywhere on the last wrong-side row. Work Eyelet Row then 3 rows of garter stitch. Bind off very loosely on the right side purlwise.

scarf finishing

Hand wash and pin out carefully to measurements. Allow to dry completely before removing pins.

stole

Cast on 88 stitches and knit 4 rows (2 garter ridges on right side).
EYELET ROW (RS) K2, *yo, k2tog; repeat from * to the last 2 stitches, k2. Work 4 rows in garter stitch, increasing one stitch on the last row—89 stitches. Begin working Twilight chart as for Scarf and continue until Stole measures 64" (162.5cm) or 1" (2.5cm) less than desired length, stretching slightly, ending with row 12 of Chart and decreasing 1 stitch by k2tog anywhere on the last wrong-side row. Work Eyelet Row, then 3 rows of garter stitch. Bind off very loosely on the right side purlwise.

stole finishing

Hand wash and pin out carefully to measurements. Allow to dry completely before removing pins.

chart

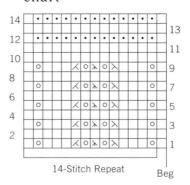

14-Stitch Repeat   Beg

key

☐ = K on RS, p on WS

· = P on RS, k on WS

⟋ = K2tog

⟍ = SSK

⅄ = Slip 1 stitch, k2tog, pass slipped stitch over

○ = Yarn over (yo)

CHAPTER FOUR

The Forest and the Trees: Scale and Perspective

There are plenty of occasions in the design process where it is beneficial to step back from the big picture and take a closer look at the individual elements of the story being told. Sometimes stripping back a complicated and busy design to a simple outline of thoughts, ideas, and details will open up new design possibilities. It's all too easy to get lost in the forest and forget to look at the trees. I sometimes get too caught up in making every available surface of a sweater a canvas for stitches when in actuality negative space can be the most effective design element. Allowing a contrast to happen naturally is a powerful visual experience.

The garments in this chapter reflect how to use space efficiently, how to match the weight of stitches and cables to a particular yarn and gauge, and how to know when to leave well enough alone while still remaining true to the conceptual vision.

portland

Designing a relatively simple cabled sweater can frequently pose more challenges for me than a more complex Aran consisting of many different cables. I surmise that part of my difficulty lies in the swatching phase, where I'm playing with cables in smaller pieces yet I'm supposed to be visualizing the entire garment. Cables can seem too small and insignificant but become more grandiose when the garment is complete and multiple repeats of the cables cover the surface.

Such was the dilemma when I designed Portland, with its wider cable panels that left little room for additional, or *secondary*, cables. It was difficult for me to limit this design to these simple elements, feeling the overall design was lacking. But once all was said and done, I loved the design and felt it has exactly the right amount of cabled activity. I did add one little bit of unusual detail in the mitered neckband. If a square neckline doesn't appeal to you, it's easy enough to simply work the neckband without the decreases for a traditional rounded neck.

Portland's name is derived from the organic yarn from Maine sheep produced by Green Mountain Spinnery and a weekend spent in Portland, Maine, with fiber friends. The shorter length lends a feminine and delicate air to this rugged sweater. The indigo colored handspun Romney along with a longer body length makes a far more masculine version.

SKILL LEVEL ○ ○ ○
Experienced

FINISHED MEASUREMENTS
CHEST 40 (44, 48, 52)" (101.5 [112, 122, 132]cm)
LENGTH 23 (24¼, 26¾, 27¼)" (58.5 [61.5, 68, 69]cm)

NOTE
Length from shoulder can be varied by 3" (7.5cm) by working more or fewer repeats of the pattern charts. (20 rows is approximately 3" [7.5cm].) Please allow extra yardage for additional length.

YARN medium
1,350 (1,450, 1,650, 1,850) yds (1,235 [1,326, 1,509, 1,692]m)

heavy worsted weight
MODEL AT LEFT Handspun Romney (100%), hand dyed dark blue
MODEL AT RIGHT 6 (6, 7, 8) skeins Green Mountain Spinnery Maine Organic, 4 oz (113.5g) skeins, each approximately 250 yds (229m), 100% certified Maine organic wool, Creamy White

NEEDLES & NOTIONS
US size 5 (3.75mm) knitting needles
US size 7 (4.5mm) knitting needles, or size needed to obtain gauge
US size 5 (3.75mm) circular needle, 16" (40cm) long
Cable needle
Stitch markers
Tapestry needle

GAUGE
16 stitches and 24 rows = 4" (10cm) in moss stitch using larger needles. Adjust needle size as necessary to obtain correct gauge.

MOSS STITCH (WORKED BACK AND FORTH)
ROW 1 (RS) (K1, p1) across.
ROWS 2 AND 4 (WS) Knit the knit stitches and purl the purl stitches as they appear.
ROW 3 (RS) (P1, k1) across.
Repeat these 4 rows for pattern.

MOSS STITCH (IN THE ROUND)
ROUNDS 1 AND 2 (K1, p1) around.
ROUNDS 3 AND 4 (P1, k1) around.
Repeat these 4 rounds for pattern.

left Handspun Romney, hand dyed right Green Mountain Spinnery Maine Organic

portland

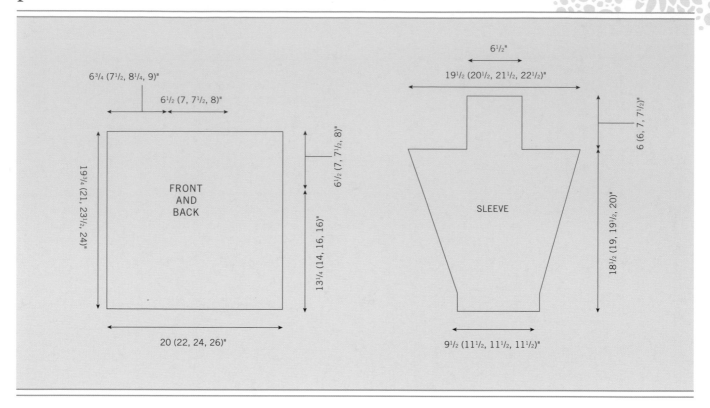

back

With smaller needles, cast on 104 (112, 120, 128) stitches.

RIBBING SETUP ROW Work (k2, p2) over 6 (10, 14, 18) stitches, ending with k2, work Chart A over 32 stitches, work Chart B over 28 stitches, work Chart A over 32 stitches, work (k2, p2) over 6 (10, 14, 18) stitches, ending with k2. Work rows 1–4 only of Charts A and B 4 (5, 4, 5) times until the piece measures approximately 2 (2½, 2, 2½)" (5 [6.5, 5, 6.5]cm), ending with row 4 of Charts.

Main Body Pattern

ROW 1 (RS) Change to larger needles. Work moss stitch over the first 6 (10, 14, 18) stitches, beginning with row 1 of Charts, work Chart A over 32 stitches, work Chart B over 28 stitches, work Chart A over 32 stitches, work moss stitch over the last 6 (10, 14, 18) stitches. Continue working all Charts until the piece measures 13¼ (14, 16, 16)" (33.5 [35.5, 40.5, 40.5]cm) from the beginning (or desired length to armhole), ending with row 8 (6, 4, 20) of Charts.

SHAPE ARMHOLES

Bind off 3 (5, 6, 6) stitches at the beginning of the next two rows. Continue in pattern as established until the armhole measures 6½ (7, 7½, 8)" (16.5 [18, 19, 20.5]cm), ending with row 8 of Charts. Bind off all stitches.

front

Work as for Back.

sleeves (MAKE 2)

With smaller needles, cast on 44 (52, 52, 52) stitches.

RIBBING SETUP ROW Work (k2, p2) over 6 (10, 10, 10) stitches, ending with k2, work Chart A over center 32 stitches, work (k2, p2) over 6 (10, 10, 10) stitches, ending with k2. Work rows 1–4 of Chart A 4 (5, 4, 5) times until the piece measures approximately 2 (2½, 2, 2½)" (5 [6.5, 5, 6.5]cm), ending with Row 4 of Chart.

Main Sleeve Pattern

ROW 1 (RS) Change to larger needles. Work moss stitch over the first 6 (10, 10, 10) stitches, beginning with row 1 of Chart, work Chart A over 32 stitches, work moss stitch over the last 6 (10, 10, 10) stitches. Continue working Chart A, increasing 1 stitch at each edge, using m1 right and left accordingly and working the new stitches into the moss stitch pattern every 4 (4, 5, 4) rows 12 (6, 20, 16) times, then every 6 rows 8 (12, 0, 6) times—84 (88, 92, 96) stitches. Work even until Sleeve measures 18½ (19, 19½, 20)" (47 [48.5, 49.5, 51]cm) from the beginning, ending with row 20 (20, 6, 6) of Chart A.

SHAPE SADDLE

Bind off 26 (28, 30, 32) stitches at the beginning of the next two rows—32 stitches. Continue to work the center 32 stitches of Chart A until the saddle measures 6 (6, 7, 7½)" (15 [15, 18, 19]cm) from the bound-off edge, ending with row 12 (12, 8, 12) of Chart A. Bind off all stitches.

finishing

Sew the long edges of the saddle along the shoulders of Front and Back. Sew the bound-off edges of Sleeves along the side edges of Front and Back. Sew side and sleeve seams.

NECKBAND

NOTE Neckband is worked in moss stitch, always working the corner stitches as knit stitches and working mitered decreases every other round.

With smaller circular needle and right side facing, begin at the left shoulder and pick up and knit 25 stitches across the saddle, 1 stitch at the corner and mark this stitch, 26 (28, 30, 32) across front neck, 1 stitch at the corner and mark, 25 stitches across the saddle, 1 stitch at the corner and mark, 26 (28, 30, 32) across back neck, 1 stitch at corner and mark—106 (110, 114, 118) stitches. Join and place marker for the beginning of round.

ROUND 1 Work in moss stitch, working all marked corner stitches as knit stitches, regardless of where they fall in the moss stitch pattern.

ROUND 2 Work to 1 stitch before the marked corner stitch, slip the next stitch and the corner stitch knitwise, knit the next stitch and pass the 2 slipped stitches over the knit stitch. Work to 1 stitch before next marked corner stitch and repeat decrease. Repeat decrease for all corners.

Repeat these 2 rounds until the neckband measures 1" (2.5cm). Bind off loosely in pattern.

Weave in all loose ends and block gently to measurements.

Handspun Romney, hand dyed

chart a

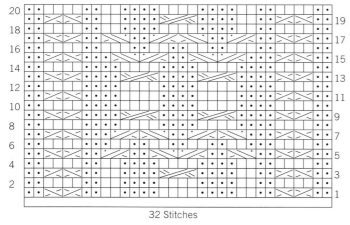

32 Stitches

chart b

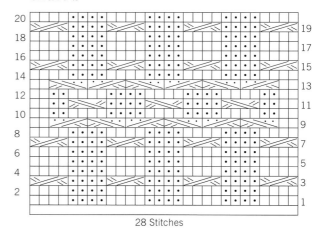

28 Stitches

key

☐ = K on RS, p on WS

· = P on RS, k on WS

= Slip next st onto cn and hold in back, k1, k1 from cn

= Slip next st onto cn and hold in front, k1, k1 from cn

= Slip next st onto cn and hold in back, k2, p1 from cn

= Slip 2 sts onto cn and hold in front, p1, k2 from cn

= Slip 2 sts onto cn and hold in back, k2, k2 from cn

= Slip 2 sts onto cn and hold in back, p2, k2, from cn

= Slip 2 sts onto cn and hold in front, k2, p2, from cn

october frost

October Frost is my homage to the oldest denizens of the forest. Those stately trees that have long since been stripped of their leaves, bark, and life's sap. They stand silent and alone, offering themselves as food and homes to birds, squirrels, raccoons, and porcupines. After November has whisked the colorful leaves of younger trees to the wind, the ageless beauty of these trunks is a testament to their integrity.

Beginning with the image of crystalline frost on a weathered brown leaf, I chose shining white mohair to blend with soft cinnamon Rambouillet/Romney crossbreed wool. The adult mohair has a larger micron count, which makes a rugged statement in this personality-filled soft yarn. This makes for a welcoming sweater-jacket for crisp, sun-filled days. Even softer to the hand is the llama and wool blend Montera from Classic Elite Yarns, with its silky halo and chunky stitch definition.

Only the boldest of cables could represent the intertwined branches of an old-growth forest. The back panel of the cardigan displays a trio of cables gracefully twining upward, flanked by knot-holed trunks. The twined trunks on the fronts have been reduced to a pair, and the sleeves feature a single, matronly tree trunk with the knothole cable continuing into the saddle.

SKILL LEVEL ◯◯◯
Experienced

FINISHED MEASUREMENTS
CHEST 39 (43, 47, 51)" (99 [109, 119.5, 129.5]cm)
LENGTH 26" (66cm)

YARN medium
1,500 (1,600, 1,750, 1,900) yds (1,372 [1,463, 1,600, 1,737m) heavy worsted weight
MODEL AT BACK Handspun Rambouillet crossbred, natural light brown (60%) and white Mohair (40%)

MODEL AT FRONT 12 (13, 14, 15) skeins Classic Elite Yarns Montera, 3½ oz (100g) skeins, each approximately 127 yds (116m), 50% llama, 50% wool, 3868 Ancient Orange

NEEDLES & NOTIONS
US size 6 (4mm) knitting needles
US size 8 (5mm) knitting needles, or size needed to obtain gauge
US size 6 (4mm) circular needle, 24" (60cm) long
Cable needle
Tapestry needle
7 buttons, 1" (2.5cm) in diameter

GAUGE
16 stitches and 24 rows = 4" (10cm) in reverse stockinette stitch using larger needles. Adjust needle size as necessary to obtain correct gauge.

K2, P2 RIBBING
ROW 1 (RS) (K2, p2) across
ROW 2 (WS) (P2, k2) across
Repeat these two rows.

REVERSE STOCKINETTE STITCH
Purl all stitches on right-side rows and knit all stitches on wrong-side rows.

back Handspun Rambouillet crossbred and Mohair front Classic Elite Yarns Montera

Handspun Rambouillet crossbred and Mohair

FOR MEN Work 2 stitches, *bind off 2 stitches, work 14 (14, 14, 14) stitches; repeat from * 6 times, bind off 2 stitches, work the last 10 stitches.
FOR BOTH Work across row, casting on 2 stitches over the bound-off stitches. Work 2 more rows of p2, k2 ribbing, then bind off loosely in pattern.

COLLAR

With smaller circular needle and right side facing, pick up and knit 94 (98, 102, 106) stitches evenly around the neck edge beginning at the front edge of Right Front, and omitting the tops of the button bands.

Beginning with right side of collar (wrong side of cardigan facing), work in k2, p2, ending with k2, until Collar measures 4 or 5" (10 or 12.5cm) or desired length. Bind off loosely in ribbing.

Sew buttons opposite buttonholes. Weave in all loose ends. Hand wash and block gently to measurements.

chart a

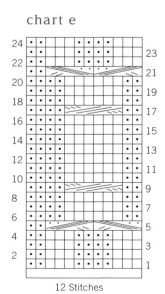

20 Stitches

chart b

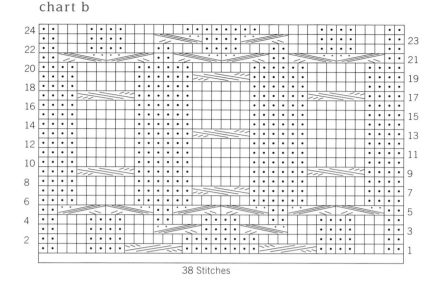

38 Stitches

chart c

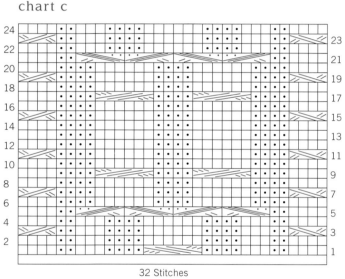

32 Stitches

chart d

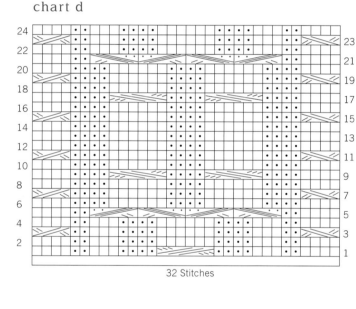

32 Stitches

chart e

chart f

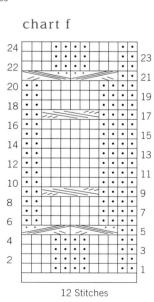

12 Stitches

12 Stitches

key

☐ = K on RS, p on WS

• = P on RS, k on WS

= Slip 2 sts to cn and hold in back, k3, p3 from cn

= Slip 3 sts to cn and hold in front, p2, k3 from cn

= Slip 3 sts onto cn and hold in back, k3, k3 from cn

= Slip 3 sts onto cn and hold in front, k3, k3 from cn

= Slip 3 sts onto cn and hold in back, k3, p3 from cn

= Slip 3 sts onto cn and hold in front, p3, k3 from cn

= Slip 2 sts onto cn and hold in back, k2, k2 from cn

= Slip 2 sts onto cn and hold in front, k2, k2 from cn

= Slip 2 sts onto cn and hold in back, k2, p2 from cn

= Slip 2 sts onto cn and hold in front, p2, k2 from cn

amanda

This pert little cardigan has become a favorite. There is something about the soothing repetition of the stitch and the bold ribbed details that seems to suit many knitters. It didn't have any high concept behind it, just an idea and simple sketch, but upon analysis it seems to me that the contrasting details of the big shawl collar and the petite silhouette make it special. Like the Town & Country cardigan (page 46), I also like to envision a longer, oversized version.

SKILL LEVEL ○○○
Intermediate Beginner

FINISHED MEASUREMENTS
CHEST 37 (40, 43, 46, 49)" (94 [101.5, 109, 117, 124.5]cm)
LENGTH 23 (24½, 25, 25½, 26)" (58.5 [62, 63.5, 65, 66]cm)

YARN medium
1,250 (1,400, 1,500, 1,650, 1,750) yds (1,143 [1,280, 1,372, 1,509, 1,600]m) heavy worsted weight
MODEL AT BACK Handspun Blue-Faced Leicester (50%) and Alpaca (50%), natural dark brown
MODEL AT FRONT 9 (10, 11, 12, 13) skeins Green Mountain Spinnery Mountain Mohair, 2 oz (57g) skeins, each approximately 140 yds (128m), 30% mohair, 70% wool, 5-BV Blue Violet

NEEDLES & NOTIONS
US size 5 (3.75mm) circular needles, 24–29" (60–74cm) long US size 7 (4.5mm) circular needles, 24–29" (60–74cm) long, or size needed to obtain gauge
One set US size 7 (4.5mm) double-pointed needles, or size needed to obtain gauge
Stitch markers
Stitch holders
Scrap yarn
Tapestry needle
7 buttons, ¾" (2cm) in diameter

GAUGE
16 stitches and 24 rows = 4" (10cm) in pattern stitch using larger needles. Adjust needle size as necessary to obtain correct gauge.

NOTE
The cardigan is worked in one piece, back and forth in rows, from the lower edge to the armhole. The Sleeves are worked separately, in rounds, then joined to the body. The upper body and upper sleeves are worked back and forth in rows in one piece, leaving a small underarm seam to join when finished. An alternate version can be worked by eliminating the shawl collar and working the narrow garter stitch edging all the way around the front edge of the cardigan.

PATTERN STITCH (WORKED BACK AND FORTH IN ROWS)
ROW 1 *K1, p2; repeat from * to end.
ROW 2 *K2, p1; repeat from * to end.
ROW 3 Knit across.
ROW 4 Purl across.
Repeat these 4 rows for pattern stitch.

PATTERN STITCH (WORKED IN THE ROUND)
ROUNDS 1 AND 2 *K1, p2; repeat from * around.
ROUNDS 3 AND 4 Knit around.
Repeat these 4 rounds for pattern stitch.

back Handspun Blue-Faced Leicester and Alpaca front Green Mountain Spinnery Mountain Mohair

amanda

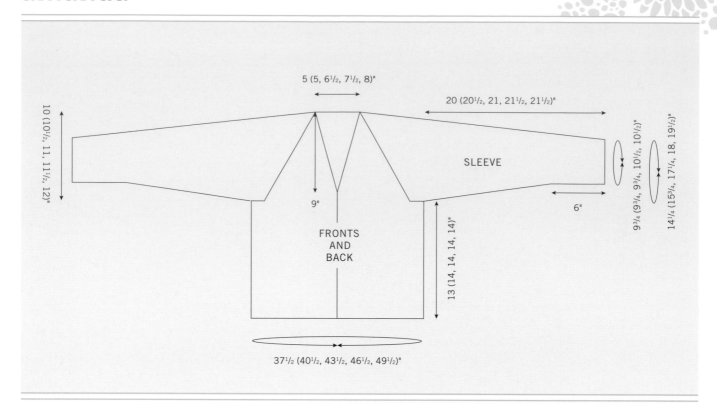

5 (5, 6½, 7½, 8)"

20 (20½, 21, 21½, 21½)"

10 (10½, 11, 11½, 12)"

9¾ (9¾, 9¾, 10½, 10½)"

14¼ (15¾, 17¼, 18, 19½)"

SLEEVE

9"

6"

FRONTS
AND
BACK

13 (14, 14, 14, 14)"

37½ (40½, 43½, 46½, 49½)"

lower body

NOTE The first and last stitch of every row is worked in stockinette stitch for selvedge stitches at the front edges.

With smaller needle, cast on 150 (162, 174, 186, 198) stitches. Work in garter stitch (knit every row) for 1" (2.5cm), ending with a wrong-side row.

Main Body Pattern

ROW 1 (RS) Change to larger needle. K1, work pattern stitch back and forth in rows over next 36 (39, 42, 45, 48) stitches for Right Front, place marker (pm), work pattern stitch over next 76 (82, 88, 94, 100) stitches for Back, pm, work pattern stitch over next 35 (38, 41, 44, 47) stitches for Left Front, end k2. Continue working pattern stitch until the piece measures 13 (14, 14, 14, 14)" (33 [35.5, 35.5, 35.5, 35.5]cm) from the beginning, or desired length to underarm, ending with row 2 of pattern stitch. Set Body aside until sleeves are completed.

sleeves (MAKE 2)

NOTE The cuff is worked with the wrong side facing because it will be folded back when worn.

With double-pointed needles, cast on 39 (39, 39, 42, 42) stitches. Place marker and join, being careful not to twist the stitches. Work in p1, k2 ribbing for 6" (15cm).

SHAPE SLEEVES

Begin working pattern stitch in rounds, increasing 1 stitch on each side of the marker, using m1 left and m1 right, accordingly, every 8 (6, 4, 4, 4) rounds 6 (7, 3, 1, 10) times, then every 10 (8, 6, 6, 6) rounds 3 (5, 12, 14, 8) times, working new stitches into pattern stitch—57 (63, 69, 72, 78) stitches, changing to larger circular needle, if necessary. Continue in pattern stitch until Sleeve measures 20 (20½, 21, 21½, 21½)" (51 [52, 53.5, 54.5, 54.5]cm), ending with row 2 of pattern stitch and ending the last round 6 stitches before the marker. Place the next 12 stitches on a holder. Place the remaining sleeve stitches on a piece of scrap yarn.

join sleeves to body

NOTE Be sure to keep continuity of pattern stitch when joining. The Sleeves are joined to Lower Body on row 3 of pattern stitch (worked back and forth). Due to the pattern stitch repeat, the underarm seam will be off pattern by one stitch.

Work across 31 (34, 37, 40, 43) stitches of Right Front, pm, place the next 12 stitches onto a holder (remove original marker), work across 45 (51, 57, 60, 66) stitches of Sleeve, pm, work across 63 (69, 75, 81, 87) Back stitches, pm, place the next 12 stitches onto a holder (remove original second marker), work across 45 (51, 57, 60, 66) stitches of Sleeve, pm, work remaining 32 (35, 38, 41, 44) stitches of Left Front— 216 (240, 264, 282, 306) stitches.

RAGLAN SHAPING

Work even in pattern stitch until the piece measures 1" (2.5cm) from the joining row.

DECREASE ROW (RS) *Work in pattern stitch until 2 stitches before marker, ssk, slip marker, k2tog; repeat from * 3 times, work in pattern stitch to end.

Work Decrease Row every other row 15 (20, 20, 21, 23) times, then every 4 rows 6 (4, 5, 5, 5) times.

At the same time, when the piece measures 14 (15½, 16, 16½, 17)" (35.5 [39.5, 40.5, 42, 43]cm), begin neck shaping.

SHAPE NECK

NECK DECREASE ROW (RS) K1, ssk, work across as established to the last 3 stitches, k2tog, k1.

Work Neck Decrease Row at neck edge every 4 (4, 2, 2, 2) rows 7 (6, 4, 9, 16) times, then every 6 (6, 4, 4, 4) rows 3 (4, 11, 9, 5) times, maintaining continuity of pattern stitch. Continue until the piece measures 23 (24½, 25, 25½, 26)" (58.5 [62, 63.5, 65, 66]cm) from the beginning, ending with a wrong-side row. Bind off remaining 20 (20, 26, 30, 32) stitches.

finishing

BUTTON BAND

With smaller needle and right side facing, pick up and knit 59 (65, 65, 67, 67) stitches along front edge beginning at the first neck decrease on Left Front. Work in garter stitch for 7 rows. Bind off loosely purlwise.

BUTTONHOLE BAND

With smaller needle and right side facing, pick up and knit 59 (65, 65, 67, 67) stitches along front edge beginning at lower edge of Right Front. Work in garter stitch for 2 rows.

BUTTONHOLE ROW Work 2 stitches, bind off next 2 stitches, *work 7 (8, 8, 8, 8) stitches, bind off 2 stitches; repeat from * 6 times, work to end. On next row, work across row, casting on 2 stitches over bound-off stitches. Work 2 more rows in garter stitch. Bind off loosely purlwise.

Collar detail in handspun Blue-Faced Leicester and Alpaca

SHAWL COLLAR

NOTE Ribbing is worked with the wrong side facing because it will be folded back when worn.

With larger circular needle and right side facing, pick up and knit 106 (106, 109, 109, 109) stitches along the neck edge, beginning and ending at the front edges of the button bands. Work in p1, k2 ribbing, and work short rows to shape collar as follows:

Work 26 (26, 27, 27, 27) stitches, pm, work 54 (54, 55, 55, 55) stitches, pm. Turn. *Work back to opposite marker, remove marker, wrap and turn (see short rows, page 152), pm. Repeat from * until all stitches are worked, ending with p1. Turn. Work in established rib for 2 rows, picking up wraps on the first row. Bind off very loosely.

Graft underarms together using Kitchener stitch (page 152). Sew buttons opposite buttonholes. Weave in all loose ends. Hand wash and block gently to measurements.

le smoking

The ladies' smoking jacket has come a long way since its invention in 1966 by Yves Saint Laurent as a feminine tuxedo jacket. The smoking jacket is now mostly thought of as a men's luxurious robe, worn by urbane gentlemen spending time lounging in a library with a good cigar and even better scotch. Who's to say that ladies can't still enjoy an incarnation of the smoking jacket as well?

For my version, I wanted the most decadent of fibers to be worn next to the skin and soft rippling cables as design elements. Limiting the placement of cables, in this case a repeating pattern that creates its own fabric, creates the contrast and allows the smooth stockinette to become a resting place for the eyes. This cardigan is also the first of several examples of what I call *organic shaping*. I like to allow cables to shape knitwear in strategic ways. In this instance, letting the cables exist at the open edges of the cardigan fronts without additional edge stitches creates a wavy edge that forms its own finish.

The charcoal Icelandic and llama blend (approximately fifty/fifty) is warm and luxurious enough for this cardigan to double as a light coat. The subtle variegation adds visual interest. The delicious Harrisville Orchid version, in a color aptly named *Claret*, is decidedly feminine and passionate at the same time.

SKILL LEVEL ○○○
Intermediate Beginner

FINISHED MEASUREMENTS
CHEST 40 (44, 46, 49)" (101.5 [112, 117, 124.5]cm)
LENGTH 26 (26½, 27, 27)" (66 [67.5, 68.5, 68.5]cm)

YARN ④ medium
1,450 (1,550, 1,700, 1,850) yds (1,326 [1,417, 1,554, 1,692]m) heavy worsted weight
MODEL AT BACK 6 (7, 7, 8) skeins Harrisville Designs Orchid with Cashmere, 3½ oz (100g) skeins, each approximately 240 yds (220m), 25% mohair, 70% fine virgin wool, 5% cashmere, 253 Claret

MODEL AT FRONT Handspun Icelandic (50%) and Llama (50%), natural dark gray

NEEDLES & NOTIONS
US size 8 (5mm) circular needle 24–29" (60–74cm) long, or size needed to obtain gauge
US size 8 (5mm) 16" (40cm) circular needle or double-pointed needles, or size needed to obtain gauge
Stitch markers
Stitch holders
Cable needle
Tapestry needle

GAUGE
16 stitches and 24 rows = 4" (10cm) in stockinette stitch. Adjust needle size as necessary to obtain correct gauge.

NOTE
The cardigan is worked in one piece, back and forth in rows, from the lower edge to the armhole. Back and Fronts are then worked separately and the shoulders are joined with a three-needle bind-off. Sleeves are picked up around the armhole edge and worked downward in rounds to the cuffs.

back Harrisville Designs Orchid with Cashmere **front** Handspun Icelandic and Llama

le smoking

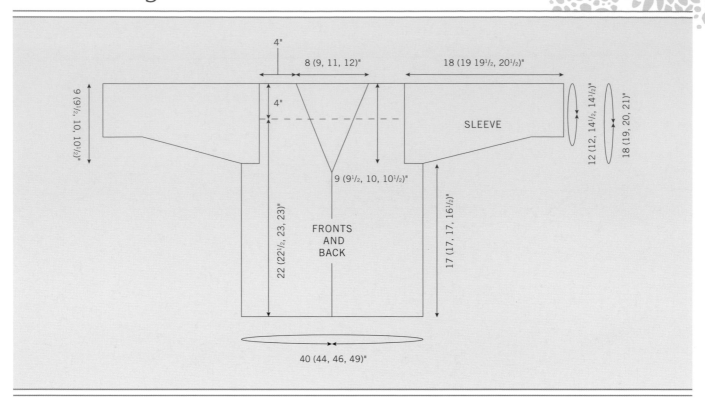

lower body

With longest circular needle, cast on 204 (216, 228, 240) stitches; do not join. Knit 2 rows, then repeat Chart over all stitches. Repeat 8 rows of Chart 3 times (24 rows), ending with row 7 of Chart on the third repeat.

NEXT ROW (WS) Work the first 24 stitches in Chart as established, place marker (pm), working in stockinette stitch, decrease 28 (24, 28, 28) stitches evenly across the next 156 (168, 180, 192) stitches using k2tog, pm, work the last 24 stitches in Chart—176 (192, 200, 212) stitches. The lower body should measure approximately 4" (10cm). Continue working Chart over the first and last 24 stitches, working stockinette stitch over the center 128 (144, 152, 164) stitches until the lower body measures 17 (17, 17, 16½)" (43 [43, 43, 42]cm) from the beginning, ending with a wrong-side row.

upper body

DIVIDE FOR BACK AND FRONTS

Work across 48 (52, 54, 57) stitches for Right Front, and place these stitches on a holder. Bind off the next 8 (10, 8, 10) stitches and work across 72 (78, 84, 88) Back stitches, and place remaining 48 (52, 54, 57) stitches on a holder for Left Front.

NEXT ROW Bind off 8 (10, 8, 10) stitches and continue working in stockinette stitch on 64 (68, 76, 78) Back stitches until Upper Back measures 5 (5½, 6, 6½)" (12.5 [14, 15, 16.5]cm) from the armhole bind-offs, ending with a wrong-side row. Bind off Back stitches.

yoke

NOTE Yoke is worked sideways with selvedge stitches for easier seaming to Upper Back and shoulders. One selvedge stitch is eliminated over the center back neck area, to allow the cables to scallop at the back neck. Cast on 26 stitches.

FIRST SHOULDER SET-UP ROW K1 (selvedge stitch), work Chart over 24 stitches, end k1 (selvedge stitch). Continue working Chart, keeping selvedge stitches in stockinette stitch, until Yoke measures 4" (10cm) from the beginning, ending with a wrong-side row.

NEXT ROW K1 (selvedge stitch), work Chart over 24 stitches, knit last two stitches together—25 stitches remain. Continue working one selvedge stitch and Chart over 24 stitches until Yoke measures 12 (13, 15, 16)" (30.5 [33, 38, 40.5]cm) from the beginning, ending with a wrong-side row.

SECOND SHOULDER SETUP ROW K1 (selvedge stitch), work across 24 stitches in Chart, increasing one stitch at the end of the row—26 stitches. Work the increased stitch as a selvedge stitch. Continue until Yoke measures 16 (17, 19, 20)" (40.5 [43, 48.5, 51]cm), ending with row 2 or 6 of Chart. Bind off all stitches.

Sew Yoke to Upper Back, with cabled edge at back neck.

right front

Place Right Front 48 (52, 54, 57) stitches on the needle, and beginning with a wrong-side row, bind off 8 (10, 8, 10) stitches and continue working in established pattern. *At the same time*, shape V-neck on the next right-side row.

SHAPE NECK

DECREASE ROW (RS) Work across first 24 stitches in Chart, ssk, work to the end of the row. Repeat Decrease Row every right—side row 4 (6, 13, 14) times then every 4 rows 9 (9, 6, 6) times—26 stitches remain for all sizes.

Continue until Right Front measures 9 (9½, 10, 10½)" (23 [24, 25.5, 26.5]cm) from the armhole bind-offs, decreasing 10 stitches evenly across the last wrong-side row. Bind off remaining 16 shoulder stitches.

left front

Place Left Front 48 (52, 54, 57) stitches on the needle, and beginning with a right-side row, bind off 8 (10, 8, 10) stitches at the beginning of the row. Continue working in established pattern and *at the same time*, begin shaping V-neck on the next right side row.

SHAPE NECK

DECREASE ROW (RS) Work across until 26 stitches remain, k2tog, work remaining 24 stitches in Chart. Repeat Decrease Row every right-side row 4 (6, 13, 14) times then every 4 rows 9 (9, 6, 6) times—26 stitches remain for all sizes.

Continue until Left Front measures 9 (9½, 10, 10½)" (23 [24, 25.5, 26.5]cm) from the armhole bind-offs, decreasing 10 stitches evenly across the last wrong-side row. Bind off remaining 16 shoulder stitches.

JOIN SHOULDERS

Sew Fronts to Back at shoulders, using the selvedge stitches on Yoke as a guide.

sleeves (MAKE 2)

With 24" (60cm) circular needle, pick up and knit 72 (76, 80, 84) stitches evenly around the armhole beginning at the underarm. Place marker for the beginning of the round at center underarm and join. Sleeves are worked in rounds in stockinette stitch until cuff.

SHAPE SLEEVE

Decrease 1 stitch on each side of the marker every 6 (6, 8, 6) rounds 5 (9, 7, 1) times, then every 8 (8, 10, 8) rounds 7 (5, 4, 12) times by working ssk at the beginning of the round and k2tog at the end of the round—48 (48, 58, 58) stitches. Change to 16" (40cm) circular and double-pointed needles as necessary. Continue until Sleeve measures 14½ (15½, 16, 17)" (37 [39.5, 40.5, 43]cm) from the beginning, increasing 12 (12, 14, 14) stitches evenly on last round—60 (60, 72, 72) stitches for the cuff. Begin repeating Chart over cuff stitches, repeating 8 rows 3 times (24 rounds), ending with row 8. Knit 2 rounds. Purl 1 round, then bind off loosely purlwise, decreasing 12 (12, 14, 14) stitches evenly around.

Belt and edging detail in Harrisville Designs Orchid with Cashmere

belt

Cast on 24 stitches. Knit 1 row, then work Chart over all stitches until belt measures 63" (160cm) or desired length. Purl 1 row, then bind off loosely purlwise.

finishing

Weave in all loose ends and block gently.

chart

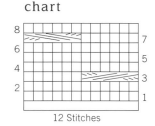

12 Stitches

key

☐ = K on RS, p on WS

⬚ = Slip 3 sts onto cn and hold in back, k3, k3 from cn

⬚ = Slip 3 sts onto cn and hold in front, k3, k3 from cn

tilly

back Green Mountain Spinnery Mountain Mohair right Rowan Felted Tweed front Handspun Churro

With so many lace scarf designs, I decided it was high time for a cabled scarf. Following the lesson I learned from the Road Not Taken scarf, I let Tilly take me on a completely new journey in design. I knew I wanted a scarf that could be worked at a multiple of gauges, from a diminutive sport/DK weight all the way up to a heavy worsted, ultra-warm version. What I didn't know was how to edge the scarf to make the flat surface that so many of us expect in neckwear. The obvious choice would have been moss or seed stitch, but the additional stitches added to the chart repeat made an extra-wide, heavy, worsted version. I threw caution to the wind and decided to let the cables do their business unassisted. I adore the result. What better accompaniment to dramatic curving cables than a softly rolled edge?

I couldn't resist exploring the contrasting theme further with the rustic handspun Churro yarn to compare with the soft and luxurious Rowan Felted Tweed at the finer gauge.

SKILL LEVEL
Intermediate

FINISHED MEASUREMENTS
SMALL Approximately 6 x 60"
(15 x 152.5cm)
LARGE Approximately 9 x 60"
(23 x 152.5cm)

YARN [3] light [4] medium
400 yds (366m) sport/DK weight
500 yds (458m) heavy worsted weight
MODEL AT BACK 4 skeins Green Mountain Spinnery Mountain Mohair, 2 oz (57g) skeins, each

approximately 140 yds (128m), 30% mohair, 70% wool, 5-SP Spice
MODEL AT RIGHT 2 skeins Rowan Felted Tweed, 1¾ oz (50g) skeins, each approximately 192 yds (175m), 50% merino, 25% alpaca, 25% viscose/rayon, 155 Pickle
MODEL AT FRONT Handspun Churro (100%), 2-ply yarn consisting of one ply natural gray and one ply light brown

NEEDLES & NOTIONS
FOR SMALL SCARF US size 4 (3.5mm) knitting needles, or size needed to obtain gauge

FOR LARGE SCARF US size 8 (5mm) knitting needles, or size needed to obtain gauge
Cable needle
Tapestry needle

GAUGE
FOR SMALL SCARF 35 stitches = 4" (10cm) in Chart patterns. Adjust needle size as necessary to obtain correct gauge.
FOR LARGE SCARF 20 stitches = 4" (10cm) in Chart patterns. Adjust needle size as necessary to obtain correct gauge.

chart a

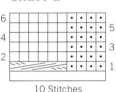

10 Stitches

chart c

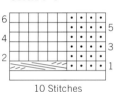

10 Stitches

scarf

Cast on 48 stitches.

First Border

ROW 1 (RS) (P4, k6) twice, p8, (k6, p4) twice.

Knit the knit stitches and purl the purl stitches as they appear for 5 more rows, ending with a wrong-side row.

Begin Charts

Work Chart A over 10 stitches, work Chart B over the center 28 stitches, end with Chart C over the last 10 stitches. Continue working Charts as established, working a total of 9 or 12 repeats of Chart B, then work an additional 8 rows of Charts.

Second Border

Work as for First Border for 4 rows, ending with a wrong-side row. Bind off loosely in pattern. Weave in all loose ends and block gently, allowing the side edges to curl.

key

☐ = K on RS, p on WS

• = P on RS, k on WS

= Slip next st to cn and hold in back, k 3, p1 from cn

= Slip 3 sts onto cn and hold in front, p1, k3 from cn

= Slip 3 sts onto cn and hold in back, k3, k3 from cn

= Slip 3 sts onto cn and hold in front, k3, k3 from cn

chart b

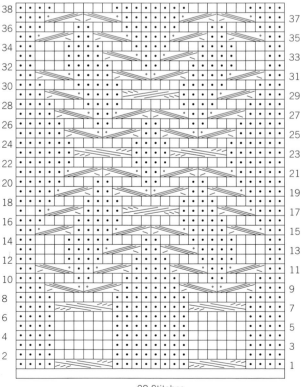

28 Stitches

saxony

These socks are another example of limiting placement of cables for maximum effect. The single Saxon braid makes a bold statement on a small canvas such as a sock. The fact that the braid also works at more than one gauge suitable for socks is a bonus. The three versions shown here illustrate how subtle changes in stitch gauge, especially over a limited surface, can completely change the look and feel of a cable. Like the Tilly scarf, it can be surprising and delightful how a cable pattern works up at a small gauge.

SKILL LEVEL ● ● ○
Intermediate

FINISHED MEASUREMENTS
SIZED TO FIT AVERAGE WOMEN'S FOOT
Leg Length 7" (18cm)
Foot Length 9½" (24cm)
Ankle Circumference 8" (20.5cm)
SIZED TO FIT AVERAGE MEN'S FOOT
Leg Length 9" (23cm)
Foot Length 10½" (26.5cm)
Ankle Circumference 8½" (21.5cm)

NOTE
The first set of numbers, in bold, refer to women's sizes; the men's sizes follow.

YARN super fine
WOMEN'S 320 (350, 370) yds (293 [320, 339]m) sock or fingering weight
MEN'S 350 (400, 470) yds (320 [366, 430]m) sock or fingering weight
MODEL AT LEFT 2 (2, 2) 2 (3, 3) skeins Lorna's Laces Yarns Shepherd Sock, 2-oz (57g) skeins, each approximately 215 yds

(197m), 80% superwash wool, 20% nylon, Denim
MODEL AT RIGHT Handspun Suffolk (100%), natural white
MODEL ON PAGE 93 2 (2, 3) 2 (3, 3) skeins Footpath Yarn, 2 oz (57g) skeins, each approximately 175 yds (160m), 85% wool, 15% nylon, Elderberry

NEEDLES & NOTIONS
One set of four double-pointed needles in US size 3 (3.25mm), 2 (2.75mm), or 1 (2.25mm), or sizes needed to obtain gauge
Cable needle
Stitch markers
Tapestry needle

GAUGE
MODEL AT LEFT 32 stitches = 4" (10cm) in stockinette stitch using US size 1 (2.25mm) needles
MODEL AT RIGHT 24 stitches = 4" (10cm) in stockinette stitch using US size 3 (3.25mm) needles
MODEL ON PAGE 93 28 stitches = 4" (10cm) in stockinette stitch using US size 2 (2.75mm) needles

Adjust needle size as necessary to obtain correct gauge.

K2, P2 RIBBING
ALL ROUNDS (K2, p2) across.

MOSS STITCH
ROUNDS 1 AND 2 (K1, p1) across.
ROUNDS 3 AND 4 (P1, k1) across.
Repeat these 4 rounds for moss stitch.

NOTE
Pattern is given in 3 different gauges. The pattern is written for the gauge obtained using US size 3 (3.25mm) needles with US size 2 (2.75mm) and US size 1 (2.25mm) needles given in parentheses. The first set of numbers, in bold, refers to the women's sock in each gauge. The second set of numbers refers to the men's sock in the three gauges. When only one number appears, it applies for all gauges.

left Lorna's Laces Yarns Shepherd Sock right Handspun Suffolk

saxony

cuff

Cast on **48 (52, 64)** 52 (60, 68) stitches loosely.
Divide stitches evenly on double-pointed needles and join. Place markers (pm) for the beginning of the round and the center of heel. Work k2, p2 ribbing for **2 (1, 1½)" (5 [2.5, 3.8]cm)** 2 (2, 1½)" (5 [5, 3.8]cm), increasing **4 (8, 8)** 4 (4, 8) stitches on last row—**52 (60, 72)** 56 (64, 76) stitches.

leg

SETUP ROW Work in moss stitch for **12 (16, 22)** 14 (18, 24) stitches, pm, p2, work Chart over 24 stitches, p2, pm, work in moss stitch for **12 (16, 22)** 14 (18, 24) stitches. Adjust the stitches around the needles for ease in working the patterns.
Continue in this manner, working **2 (4, 4)** 3 (5, 5) repeats of Chart. The leg should measure approximately **7" (18cm)** 9" (23cm) from the beginning.
NEXT ROUND Knit across all stitches, decreasing **4 (8, 8)** 4 (4, 8) stitches evenly across the round—**48 (52, 64)** 52 (60, 68) stitches.

HEEL FLAP

ROW 1 (RS) Work **12 (13, 16)** 13 (15, 17) stitches from the center of heel marker. Turn.
ROW 2 Slip 1 stitch purlwise, purl **11 (12, 15)** 12 (14, 16) stitches, slip the center of heel marker, purl **12 (13, 16)** 13 (15, 17) stitches—**24 (26, 32)** 26 (30, 34) heel stitches. Leave remaining **24 (26, 32)** 26 (30, 34) stitches unworked for the instep.
ROW 3 Slip 1 stitch purlwise, (k1, p1) across, ending with k1.
ROW 4 Slip 1 stitch purlwise, purl to end.
Repeat rows 3 and 4 until heel flap measures **2" (5cm)** 2½" (6.5cm).

TURN HEEL

Note Slip the first stitch of every row purlwise.
ROW 1 (RS) Knit **14 (15, 18)** 15 (17, 19), ssk, k1. Turn.
ROW 2 Slip 1, p5, p2tog, p1. Turn.
ROW 3 Slip 1, k6, ssk, k1. Turn.
ROW 4 Slip 1, p7, p2tog, p1. Turn.
Continue in this manner, working to 1 stitch before the gap, then work this stitch together with the stitch after the gap, until all heel stitches have been worked, ending with a wrong-side row.

HEEL GUSSET

Note Foot is worked in stockinette stitch.
Work **7 (8, 9)** 8 (9, 10) stitches to the marked stitch for the beginning of round, knit the second half of the heel stitches, pick up **13 (14, 17)** 14 (16, 18) stitches along the side of the heel, place first marker, work across **24 (26, 32)** 26 (30, 34) instep stitches, place second marker, pick up **13 (14, 17)** 14 (16, 18) stitches along the side of the heel, work across the remaining **7 (8, 9)** 8 (9, 10) heel stitches—**64 (70, 84)** 70 (80, 90) stitches.

Handspun Suffolk

SHAPE GUSSET

DECREASE ROUND Work to 3 stitches before the first marker, k2tog, k1, work to second marker, k1, ssk, work to the beginning of round marker.
NEXT ROUND Work even.
Repeat these 2 rounds until **48 (52, 64)** 52 (60, 68) stitches remain.

foot

Continue working in rounds until foot measures **8" (20.5cm)** 9" (23cm) or 2" (5cm) less than the desired length, ending at the beginning of round marker.

SHAPE TOE

ROUND 1 Work to 4 stitches before the first marker, k2tog, k2, k2, ssk, work to 4 stitches before the second marker, k2tog, k2, k2, ssk, work to the beginning of round marker.
ROUND 2 Work even.
Repeat these 2 rounds until **24 (28, 32)** 28 (32, 36) stitches remain. Work round 1 only until **12 (16, 16)** 12 (16, 16) stitches remain.

finishing

Divide remaining stitches evenly on two needles. Graft the stitches together using Kitchener stitch (page 152).
Weave in ends on inside of sock.

The Saxony braided cable in Lorna's Laces (Denim) and Footpath Yarn (Elderberry).

chart

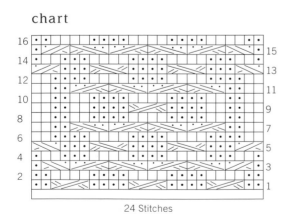

24 Stitches

key

☐ = K on RS, p on WS

• = P on RS, k on WS

= Slip next st onto cn and hold in back, k2, p1 from cn

= Slip 2 sts onto cn and hold in front, p1, k2 from cn

= Slip 2 sts onto cn and hold in back, k2, p2 from cn

= Slip 2 sts onto cn and hold in front, p2, k2 from cn

= Slip 2 sts onto cn and hold in back, k2, k2 from cn

= Slip 2 sts onto cn and hold in front, k2, k2 from cn

narragansett bay

While working on this book, I had an opportunity to spend some all-too-brief time in the wonderful town of Newport, Rhode Island. This is a town rich in contrasts of old and new, and this juxtaposition played nicely with the contrasting themes running through my head at the time. Even more dramatic was a tourist harbor cruise, where I saw some of the world's fastest racing boats, America's Cup winners, luxurious yachts, antique schooners, and working lobster boats all in one tiny space of water. All of the images, including the amazing mansions on the shore and lighthouses dotted about, filled me with design inspiration. However, the only boat my heart yearned for was the lobster boat returning from a morning's catch, and I desperately wanted to join the couple aboard and really feel what it's like to do a hard day's work. I was reminded again of the knitting heritage of fishing ganseys and the romantic vision of lassies knitting dockside while waiting for their loved ones to return from the sea.

It seemed fitting to design the Narragansett Bay set for both men and women, and to include pieces that could actually be useful out on the Atlantic. While the exquisite natural white set is far too delicate for fishing, it is a beautiful showcase for the traditional stitchwork. I chose the gansey motif to represent the Claiborne Pell Bridge, the longest suspension bridge in New England, which crosses Narragansett Bay to the island that houses Newport.

The hand-dyed Lorna's Laces yarns are superwash wool, which I always find useful for things like hats and scarves. The ultra-soft Cormo wool is pure and untouched for the cap and scarf, but the wool for the socks was blended with 25 percent nylon for additional strength.

These pieces posed more of a design challenge than initially meets the eye. Once I chose a traditional gansey motif, I needed to be sure it fit within the sizes, gauges, and other restrictions I placed upon the project. This involved lots of swatching to determine the various gauges for the three weights of yarn and manipulating the chart to best fit within all the spaces necessary. Changing direction was also needed for the cuff-down knitting of the socks and to make the scarf symmetrical. It was indeed a fun project and a great learning experience for me as a designer. And yes, I do have fantasies of turning this design into a full-blown gansey sweater.

cap at top Handspun Cormo Wool cap at right Lorna's Laces Yarns Shepherd Worsted scarf at left Lorna's Laces Yarns Shepherd Sport
scarf at right Handspun Cormo Wool

narragansett bay socks

SKILL LEVEL ● ● ○
Intermediate

**FINISHED
MEASUREMENTS**
**SIZED TO FIT AVERAGE
WOMEN'S FOOT**
Leg Length 7" (18cm)
Foot Length 9½" (24cm)
Ankle Circumference 8" (20.5cm)
SIZED TO FIT AVERAGE MEN'S FOOT
Leg Length 9" (23cm)
Foot Length 10½" (26.5cm)
Ankle Circumference 8½"
(21.5cm)

YARN **super fine**
WOMEN'S 350 yds (320m) sock
or fingering weight
MEN'S 450 yds (412m) sock or
fingering weight
MODEL AT TOP 2 (3) skeins
Lorna's Laces Yarns Shepherd
Sock, 2 oz (57g) skeins, each
approximately 215 yds (197m),
80% superwash wool, 20% nylon,
Cranberry
MODEL AT BOTTOM Handspun
Cormo Wool (75%) and Nylon
(25%), natural white

NEEDLES & NOTIONS
One set of 5 US size 1 (2.25mm)
double-pointed needles, or size
needed to obtain gauge
Stitch markers
Tapestry needle

GAUGE
32 stitches = 4" (10cm) in
seed stitch. Adjust needle
size as necessary to obtain
correct gauge.

SEED STITCH
ROUND 1 (K1, p1) around.
ROUND 2 (P1, k1) around.
Repeat these 2 rounds for
pattern.

NOTE
The first set of numbers refers to
the women's sock. The men's sock
numbers follow in parentheses.

cuff

Cast on 64 (68) stitches loosely.

Divide stitches evenly on double-pointed needles and join. Place
marker for the beginning of round. The beginning of the round will be at
the side of the sock. Work in seed stitch for 1 (1)" (2.5 [2.5]cm). Knit
one round.

leg

SET UP LEG Work seed stitch over 2 (3) stitches, work Chart A over 28
(28) stitches, work seed stitch over 4 (6) stitches, work Chart A over 28
(28) stitches, work seed stitch over the last 2 (3) stitches.
Continue in this manner until the leg measures approximately 7 (9)" (18
[23]cm) in length, ending with row 18 of Chart A.

HEEL FLAP
ROW 1 (RS) Knit across 32 (34) stitches for the heel flap. Leave
remaining 32 (34) stitches unworked for the instep. Place a marker
after 16 (17) stitches for the center of heel. Turn.
ROW 2 (WS) Slip 1 stitch purlwise, purl to end.
ROW 3 (Slip 1 stitch purlwise, k1) across.
ROW 4 Slip 1 stitch purlwise, purl to end.
Repeat rows 3 and 4 until the heel flap measures 2 (2½)" (5 [6.5]cm).

TURN HEEL
Note Slip the first stitch of every row purlwise.
ROW 1 (RS) K18 (19), ssk, k1. Turn.
ROW 2 Slip 1, p5, p2tog, p1. Turn.
ROW 3 Slip 1, k6, ssk, k1. Turn.
ROW 4 Slip 1, p7, p2tog, p1. Turn.
Continue in this manner, working to 1 stitch before the gap, then work
this stitch together with the stitch after the gap, until all heel stitches
have been worked, ending with a wrong-side row.
NOTE Chart A continues down the instep of the sock while the foot is
worked in stockinette stitch.

HEEL GUSSET

ROW 1 Work across 18 (20) stitches of the heel, pick up 16 (18)
stitches along the side of the heel, place first marker, work across 32
(34) instep stitches in established pattern removing beginning of round
marker, place second marker, pick up 16 (18) stitches along the side of
the heel, knit across to the center of heel marker.

SHAPE GUSSET
DECREASE ROUND Work to 3 stitches before first marker, k2tog, k1. Work
in pattern as established until second marker, k1, ssk, work to end.
NEXT ROUND Work even.
Repeat these 2 rounds until 64 (68) stitches remain.

foot

Continue working in rounds until the foot measures 8 (9)" (20.5
[23]cm) or 2 (2)" (2.5 [2.5]cm) less than the desired length, ending at
the center of heel marker.

SHAPE TOE
ROUND 1 Work to 4 stitches before the first marker, k2tog, k2, k2, ssk,
work to 4 stitches before the second marker, k2tog, k2, k2, ssk, work
to end.
ROUND 2 Work even.
Repeat these 2 rounds until 32 (36) stitches remain. Work round 1
only until 16 stitches remain.

finishing

Divide remaining the stitches evenly on two needles. Graft stitches
together using Kitchener stitch (page 152).
Weave in ends on inside of sock.

op Lorna's Laces Yarns Shepherd Sock bottom Handspun Cormo wool and nylon

narragansett bay cap

SKILL LEVEL ○○○
Intermediate Beginner

FINISHED MEASUREMENTS
Circumference 21 (23)" (53.5 [58.5]cm)

YARN ⓵ light
110 (130) yds (101 [119]m) worsted weight
MODEL AT TOP Handspun Cormo Wool (100%), natural white
MODEL AT RIGHT 1 (1) skein Lorna's Laces Yarns Shepherd Worsted, 4 oz (113.5g) skeins, each approximately 225 yds (206m), 100% superwash wool, Cranberry

NEEDLES & NOTIONS
US size 5 (3.75mm) circular needle 16" (40cm) long, or size needed to obtain gauge
One set US size 5 (3.75mm) double-pointed needles, or size needed to obtain gauge
Stitch marker
Tapestry needle

GAUGE
20 stitches and 28 rows = 4" (10cm) in seed stitch. Adjust needle size as necessary to obtain correct gauge.

SEED STITCH
ROUND 1 (K1, p1) around.
ROUND 2 (P1, k1) around.
Repeat these 2 rounds for pattern.

hat
With circular needle, cast on 102 (114) stitches and join, placing marker for the beginning of round. Work in seed stitch for 1 (1)" (2.5 [2.5]cm). Knit one round.
SET-UP ROUND *Work Chart C over 28 stitches, work seed stitch over 6 (10) stitches; repeat from * twice more. Work 18 rounds of Chart C. Knit 1 round. Work seed stitch for 1 (1)" (2.5 [2.5]cm), then work in stockinette stitch for 1½ (1½)" (3.8 [3.8]cm). Hat should measure 5 (5)" (12.5 [12.5]cm). Knit one round, decreasing 8 (2) stitches evenly around—94(112) stitches remain.

SHAPE CAP
Note Change to double-pointed needles as necessary.
ROUND 1 (K2, k2tog) around.
ROUNDS 2 AND 3 Knit.
ROUND 4 (K1, k2tog) around.
ROUNDS 5 AND 6 Knit.
ROUND 7 K2tog around.
ROUNDS 8 AND 9 Knit.
ROUNDS 10 AND 11 K2tog around.

finishing
Cut yarn and draw through last stitches with a tapestry needle. Knot securely. Weave in all loose ends.

chart a, for socks

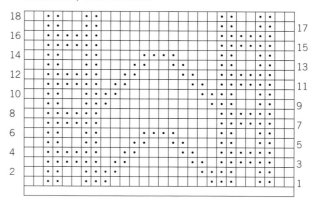

28 Stitches

narragansett bay scarf

SKILL LEVEL ○○○
Intermediate Beginner

FINISHED
MEASUREMENTS
Approximately 8½ x 54" (21.5 x
137cm)

YARN **2** fine
400 yds (366m) sport weight
MODEL AT LEFT 2 skeins Lorna's
Laces Yarns Shepherd Sport,
2½-oz (74g) skeins, each
approximately 200 yds (183m),
100% superwash wool, Cranberry
MODEL AT RIGHT Handspun Cormo
Wool (100%), natural white

NEEDLES & NOTIONS
US size 4 (3.5mm) knitting
    needles, or size needed to
    obtain gauge
Tapestry needle

GAUGE
24 stitches = 4" (10cm) in seed
stitch. Adjust needle size as
necessary to obtain correct gauge.

SEED STITCH
ROW 1 (K1, p1) across
ALL OTHER ROWS Knit the purl
stitches and purl the knit stitches
as they appear.

scarf

Cast on 58 stitches and work seed stitch for 1" (2.5cm), ending with a right-side row.

NEXT ROW (WS) Work seed stitch over 6 stitches, purl 46 stitches, work seed stitch over the last 6 stitches.

NEXT ROW (RS) Work seed stitch over 6 stitches, work Chart B over 46 stitches, work seed stitch over the last 6 stitches. Continue until scarf measures 53" (134.5cm), ending with row 18 of Chart B. Work seed stitch over all stitches for 1" (2.5cm). Bind off loosely in pattern.

finishing

Weave in all loose ends and block flat.

chart b, for scarf

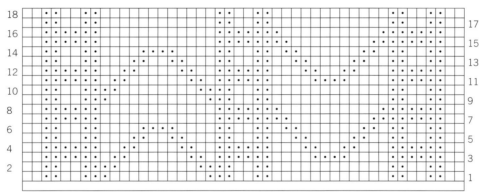

46 Stitches

chart c, for cap

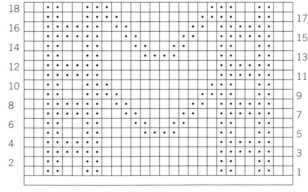

28 Stitches

key

☐ = K on RS, p on WS

⊡ = P on RS, k on WS

CHAPTER FIVE

Conceptual Stitches and Emotive Design

In this chapter, we arrive at a group of high-concept designs that expand upon the themes explored in the previous two chapters. There are still contrasts with color, fiber, and stitches, but now I've added some additional themes to give the designs enhanced richness and meaning. The first group of patterns represents somewhat literal concepts within the stitches and garments themselves. The second group has a more abstract vision, with meticulous fiber design of color and texture.

CONCEPTUAL STITCHES

I find Aran knitting to be particularly responsive to developing a conceptual sweater. There is generally a good amount of space in which to place a variety of cables to tell a story. Like ensemble music, the individual rhythm and balance of each cable plays a role in the overall picture, and when taken in all together, the viewer will hopefully become lost within the vision.

When designing a conceptual Aran, I start with the central theme and choose cables that I feel best represent the concept at hand. Sometimes I begin with the largest, which is often the center motif (but not always), and sometimes a smaller secondary cable catches my eye and begins the story. There are times that I group and configure cables based on pure instinct, but there are other times when I utilize a more mathematical and logical approach.

The lace pieces in this group serve more as vintage-inspired and ladylike garments of the 1940s and 1950s—a time when a Shetland cardigan was often teamed with a wool plaid skirt for daywear. Ruby (page 118) and Harriet (page 124) began their lives as a twinset in my mind, but they started to take on individual lives of their own, so I let the designs establish their own voices. I still like to think of them together and, while they may not have quite the vintage appeal that I originally intended, they are certainly still fashion-forward when paired together.

EMOTIVE DESIGN

Although I don't believe that all knitwear needs to serve a higher purpose other than to be functional, I sometimes feel the need to express myself in a more conceptual manner. The designs beginning with Gaelic Mist (page 130) are personal expressions of natural wonders and emotions. Like any storyteller, my vision is the beginning of a story that only you, the viewer, can finish.

halcyon

I would like to say that Halcyon holds a special place in my heart, but all my Aran designs are special to me because they are all so conceptual and emotive. Having said that, Halcyon really does have a piece of my heart. I set out to make an Aran that was symmetrical, balanced, and exceptionally pleasing and restful to the eye, and it certainly pleases me in whatever yarn I choose for it. I deliberately did not crowd the canvas with too many cables. Instead, I chose cables that entwine in unusual ways and played with the contrast of circular and rectilinear motifs because I think that certain contrasting images form a perfect balance together.

The California Red wool in the handspun version is beautiful and its perfect simplicity is a wonderful backdrop for this sweater.

SKILL LEVEL ○ ○ ○
Experienced

FINISHED MEASUREMENTS
CHEST 40 (42, 45, 47, 50)" (101.5 [106.5, 114.5, 119.5, 127]cm)
LENGTH 26½" (67.5cm)

YARN medium
1,450 (1,550, 1,650, 1,850, 1,950) yds (1,326 [1,417, 1,509, 1,692, 1,783]m) worsted weight
MODEL AT BACK 7 (8, 8, 9, 9) skeins Black Water Abbey Yarns Worsted Weight, 4 oz (114 g) skeins, each approximately 220 yds (201m), 100% wool, Bluestack

MODEL AT FRONT Handspun California Red (100%), natural white

NEEDLES & NOTIONS
US size 5 (3.75mm) knitting needles
US size 7 (4.5mm) knitting needles, or size needed to obtain gauge
US size 5 (3.75mm) circular needle, 16" (40cm) long
Cable needle
Stitch holders
Tapestry needle

GAUGE
18 stitches and 30 rows = 4" (10cm) in reverse stockinette stitch using larger needles. Adjust needle size as necessary to obtain correct gauge.

back Black Water Abbey Yarns Worsted Weight front Handspun California Red

halcyon

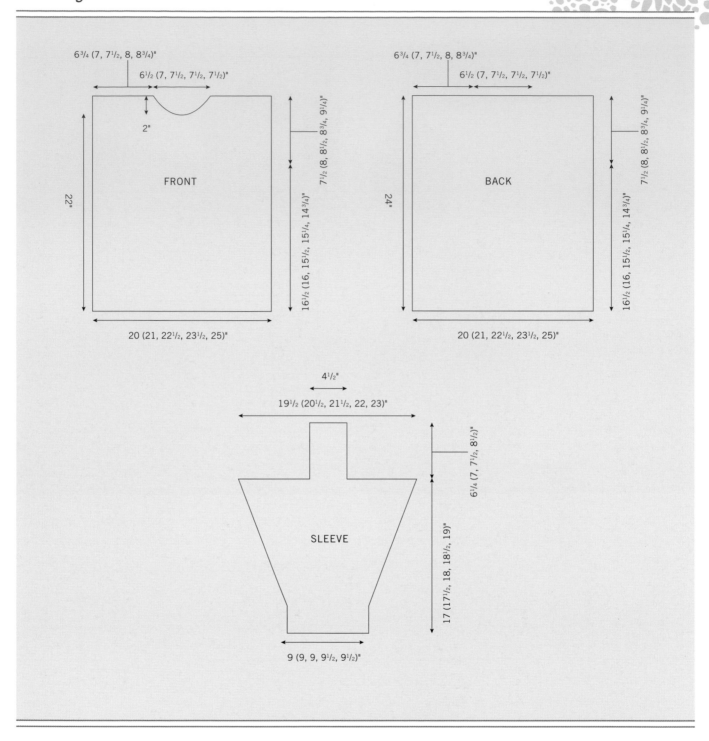

FRONT

6³/₄ (7, 7¹/₂, 8, 8³/₄)"

6¹/₂ (7, 7¹/₂, 7¹/₂, 7¹/₂)"

2"

22"

7¹/₂ (8, 8¹/₂, 8³/₄, 9¹/₄)"

16¹/₂ (16, 15¹/₂, 15¹/₄, 14³/₄)"

20 (21, 22¹/₂, 23¹/₂, 25)"

BACK

6³/₄ (7, 7¹/₂, 8, 8³/₄)"

6¹/₂ (7, 7¹/₂, 7¹/₂, 7¹/₂)"

24"

7¹/₂ (8, 8¹/₂, 8³/₄, 9¹/₄)"

16¹/₂ (16, 15¹/₂, 15¹/₄, 14³/₄)"

20 (21, 22¹/₂, 23¹/₂, 25)"

SLEEVE

4¹/₂"

19¹/₂ (20¹/₂, 21¹/₂, 22, 23)"

6¹/₄ (7, 7¹/₂, 8¹/₂)"

17 (17¹/₂, 18, 18¹/₂, 19)"

9 (9, 9, 9¹/₂, 9¹/₂)"

back

With smaller needles, cast on 114 (118, 126, 130, 138) stitches.

Ribbing Setup Row

SIZES 40, 47, AND 50 ONLY (K2, p2) 5 (7, 8) times, work row 1 of Chart A, p2, (k2, p2) 3 times, work row 1 of Chart B, p2, (k2, p2) 7 times, work row 1 of Chart A, p2, (k2, p2) 3 times, work row 1 of Chart B, p2, (k2, p2) 4 (6, 7) times, k2.

SIZES 42 AND 45 ONLY P2, (k2, p2) 5 (6) times, work row 1 of Chart A, p2, (k2, p2) 3 times, work row 1 of Chart B, p2, (k2, p2) 7 times, work row 1 of Chart A, p2, (k2, p2) 3 times, work row 1 of Chart B, p2, (k2, p2) 5 (6) times.

ALL SIZES Continue working patterns as established until the ribbing measures 3" (7.5cm), ending with row 4 of Charts.

Main Body Pattern

ROW 1 (RS) Change to larger needles. P2 (4, 8, 10, 14) stitches, work Chart C over 16 stitches, p2, work Chart A over 4 stitches, p2, work Chart D over 10 stitches, p2, work Chart B over 4 stitches, p2, work Chart E over 26 stitches, p2, work Chart A over 4 stitches, p2, work Chart F over 10 stitches, p2, work Chart B over 4 stitches, p2, work Chart C over 16 stitches, p2 (4, 8, 10, 14).

Continue working all Charts until 6 repeats of Chart E are complete. Back measures 24" (61cm). Bind off all stitches.

front

Work same as for Back until 5 repeats of Chart E are complete, then work 16 more rows of Charts.

SHAPE FRONT NECK

Keeping continuity of Charts, work across 42 (43, 45, 47, 51) stitches for the left shoulder. Join a second ball of yarn and work across center 30 (32, 36, 36, 36) stitches and place on holder for front neck, work across remaining 42 (43, 45, 47, 51) stitches for the right shoulder. Using two balls of yarn and working both sides at same time, decrease 1 stitch at each neck edge on every right-side row 4 times as follows: Work across first shoulder until 3 stitches remain, k2tog, k1 (for neck selvedge). For second shoulder, k1 (for neck selvedge), ssk, work to end—38 (39, 41, 43, 47) stitches for each shoulder. Work even until Front measures same length as Back. Bind off shoulder stitches.

sleeves (MAKE 2)

With smaller needles, cast on 46 (46, 46, 50, 50) stitches.

Ribbing Setup Row

SIZES 40, 42, AND 45 ONLY P2, (k2, p2) 2 times, work row 1 of Chart B, p2, (k2, p2) 4 times, work row 1 of Chart A, p2, (k2, p2) 2 times.

SIZES 47 AND 50 ONLY (K2, p2) 3 times, work row 1 of Chart B, p2, (k2, p2) 4 times, work row 1 of Chart A, p2, (k2, p2) 2 times, k2.

ALL SIZES Continue working in pattern as established until ribbing measures 3" (7.5cm), ending with row 3 of Charts A and B. On next row, work in pattern as established and increase 2 stitches evenly between cables using the m1 method—48 (48, 48, 52, 52) stitches.

Main Sleeve Pattern

ROW 1 (RS) Change to larger needles. P10 (10, 10, 12, 12), work Chart B, p2, work Chart C, p2, work Chart A, p10 (10, 10, 12, 12). Continue working Charts, increasing 1 stitch at each edge using m1 left and m1 right accordingly, working new stitches in reverse stockinette stitch, every 4 rows 24 (26, 28, 28, 30) times—96 (100, 104, 108, 112) stitches. Work even until Sleeve measures 17 (17½, 18, 18½, 19)" (43 [44.5, 45.5, 47, 48.5]cm) from the beginning, ending with a wrong-side row.

Black Water Abbey Yarns Worsted Weight

SHAPE SADDLE

Bind off 33 (35, 37, 39, 41) stitches on the next row, work Chart B as established, p2tog, work Chart C as established, p2tog, work Chart A as established, work to the end of the row.

NEXT ROW Bind off 33 (35, 37, 39, 41) stitches, work to the end of the row—30 stitches for saddle with only 1 reverse stockinette stitch between Charts. Work even on saddle stitches, keeping continuity of Charts, until the saddle measures approximately 6¾ (7¼, 7¾, 8½, 9)" (17 [18.5, 19.5, 21.5, 23]cm) in length, ending with row 12 of Chart C, slightly stretching the saddle, if necessary. Bind off all stitches.

finishing

Sew the long edges of the saddles along the shoulders of Front and Back. Sew bound-off edges of Sleeves along the side edges of Front and Back. Sew side and sleeve seams.

NECKBAND

With smaller circular needle and beginning at left side of Back, pick up 96 (100, 104, 104, 108) stitches evenly around the neck edge, including the front neck stitches on the holder. Place marker for the beginning of round and join. Work in k2, p2 rib for 1½" (3.8cm). Bind off loosely in pattern.

Weave in all loose ends and block gently to measurements.

back Black Water Abbey Yarns Worsted Weight front Handspun California Red

chart a

4 Stitches

chart b

4 Stitches

chart c

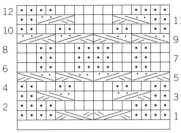

16 Stitches

chart d

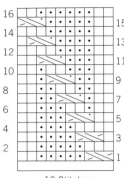

10 Stitches

chart e

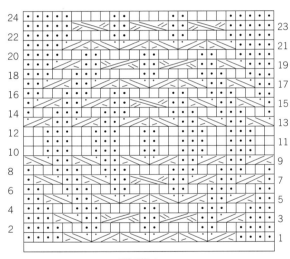

26 Stitches

chart f

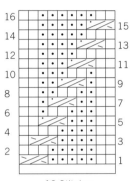

10 Stitches

key

☐ = K on RS, p on WS

⊡ = P on RS, k on WS

= Slip next st onto cn and hold in back, k2, p1 from cn

= Slip 2 sts onto cn and hold in front, p1, k2 from cn

= Slip 2 sts onto cn and hold in front, k1, k2 from cn

= Slip 2 sts onto cn and hold in back, k2, k2 from cn

= Slip 2 sts onto cn and hold in front, k2, k2 from cn

= Slip 2 sts onto cn and hold in back, k2, p2 from cn

= Slip 2 sts onto cn and hold in front, p2, k2 from cn

st. patrick

Inspired by the conceptual designs of Alice Starmore, I tested my own design waters more than ten years ago with St. Patrick, my first but never published design. I chose cables that, in my mind, represent both the myth and the man who was St. Patrick. Snakelike cables were obvious motifs to use, and the more complex and interwoven cables are meant to symbolize Celtic art and the complexity of faith.

The handspun yarn was a joy to design using multiple colors of mohair blended with emerald green wool. I wanted a jeweled, heathery yarn like wildflowers in an Irish field. The goal ratio for the yarn was 75 percent wool and 25 percent Mohair. The green wool is a result of 75 percent of the wool being dyed dark forest green and 25 percent dyed bright lime. The mohair was dyed in five separate colors: royal blue, dark purple, magenta, bronze gold, and a sunny yellow. The carding process took a long time as I fed varying amounts of fiber into the drum carder until I had a batt that resembled the final goal. I carded all the fiber by eye, then stripped the batts and carded and recarded them for consistency. I admit that this was not the most time-efficient method for carding fiber, and I revised my method for other projects later in this chapter. However, the yarn is exactly as I envisioned. But what is even better? The Romney/Border Leicester wool came from a sheep named Patrick. You can't get more conceptual than that!

SKILL LEVEL ○ ○ ○
Experienced

FINISHED MEASUREMENTS
CHEST 40 (44, 47, 51)" (101.5 [112, 119.5, 129.5]cm)
LENGTH 23 (23, 28, 28)" (58.5 [58.5, 71, 71]cm)
Note Length can be adjusted by 5" (12.5cm), or one 36-row repeat of Chart B. Please allow extra yardage for longer length.

YARN medium
1,400 (1,500, 1,800, 1,950) yds (1,280 [1,372, 1,646, 1,783]m) worsted weight
MODEL AT LEFT Handspun Romney/ Border Leicester crossbred (75%) and Mohair (25%), hand dyed dark green heather
MODEL AT RIGHT 4, 8 (8, 10, 11) skeins Rowan Yarns Scottish Tweed Aran, 3½-oz (100g) skeins, each approximately 186 yds (170m), 100% pure new wool, 024 Porridge

NEEDLES & NOTIONS
US size 5 (3.75mm) knitting needles
US size 7 (4.5mm) knitting needles, or size needed to obtain gauge
US size 5 (3.75mm) circular needles, 16" (40cm) long
Cable needle
Stitch holders
Tapestry needle

GAUGE
18 stitches and 28 rows = 4" (10cm) over box stitch using larger needles. Adjust needle size as necessary to obtain correct gauge.

BOX STITCH
ROW 1 (RS) *K2, p2; repeat from *, end k2.
ROWS 2 AND 3 *P2, k2; repeat from *, end p2.
ROW 4 *K2, p2; repeat from *, end k2.
Repeat these 4 rows for pattern.

left Handspun Romney/Border Leicester crossbred and mohair, hand dyed right Rowan Yarns Scottish Tweed Aran

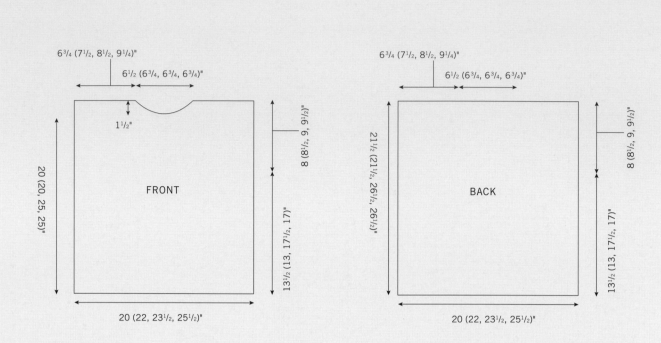

6³/₄ (7¹/₂, 8¹/₂, 9¹/₄)"

6¹/₂ (6³/₄, 6³/₄, 6³/₄)"

1¹/₂"

8 (8¹/₂, 9, 9¹/₂)"

FRONT

20 (20, 25, 25)"

13¹/₂ (13, 17¹/₂, 17)"

20 (22, 23¹/₂, 25¹/₂)"

6³/₄ (7¹/₂, 8¹/₂, 9¹/₄)"

6¹/₂ (6³/₄, 6³/₄, 6³/₄)"

8 (8¹/₂, 9, 9¹/₂)"

BACK

21¹/₂ (21¹/₂, 26¹/₂, 26¹/₂)"

13¹/₂ (13, 17¹/₂, 17)"

20 (22, 23¹/₂, 25¹/₂)"

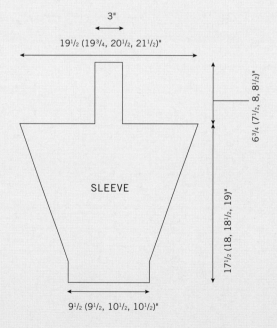

3"

19¹/₂ (19³/₄, 20¹/₂, 21¹/₂)"

6³/₄ (7¹/₂, 8, 8¹/₂)"

SLEEVE

17¹/₂ (18, 18¹/₂, 19)"

9¹/₂ (9¹/₂, 10¹/₂, 10¹/₂)"

back

With smaller needles, cast on 116 (126, 131, 141) stitches. Work the 5-stitch repeat of Chart A across, ending with k1. Continue until the piece measures 2½" (6.5cm), ending with row 5 of Chart A.

NEXT ROW (WS) Purl across, increasing 4 (2, 5, 3) stitches evenly across row using the m1 method—120 (128, 136, 144) stitches.

Main Body Pattern

ROW 1 (RS) Change to larger needles. Work box stitch over 10 (14, 18, 22) stitches, work Chart B over 18 stitches, work Chart C over 8 stitches, work Chart D over 48 stitches, work Chart E over 8 stitches, work Chart B over 18 stitches, work box stitch over 10 (14, 18, 22) stitches. Continue working all Charts until Back measures 21½ (21½, 26½, 26½)" (54.5 [54.5, 67.5, 67.5]cm) from the beginning, ending with row 26 of Chart B and row 6 of all other Charts. Bind off all stitches.

front

Work as for Back until Front measures 20 (20, 25, 25)" (51 [51, 63.5, 63.5]cm) from the beginning, ending with row 10 of Chart D.

SHAPE FRONT NECK

Work across 44 (47, 50, 53) stitches for shoulder, place center 32 (34, 36, 38) stitches on holder for front neck, join a new ball of yarn and work to the end of the row. Using 2 balls of yarn and working both sides at the same time, decrease 1 stitch at each neck edge every other row 4 (4, 3, 4) times as follows: Work across first shoulder until 3 stitches remain, k2tog, k1 (for neck selvedge). For second shoulder, k1 (for neck selvedge), ssk, work to end—40 (43, 47, 49) stitches for each shoulder. Work even until Front measures same length as Back, ending with row 26 of Chart B and row 6 of all other Charts. Bind off all stitches.

sleeves (MAKE 2)

With smaller needles, cast on 50 (50, 55, 55) stitches. Work the 5-stitch repeat of Chart A across. Continue until the piece measures 2½" (6.5cm), ending with row 5 of Chart A.

NEXT ROW (WS) Purl across, increasing 12 (12, 7, 7) stitches evenly across row using the m1 method—62 stitches.

Main Sleeve Pattern

ROW 1 (RS) Change to larger needles. Work Chart F over 22 stitches, work Chart G over 18 stitches, work Chart F over 22 stitches. Continue working Charts, increasing 1 stitch at each edge every 4 rows 13 (15, 19, 23) times, then every 6 rows 8 (7, 5, 3) times, using m1 left and right accordingly, and working the new stitches in box stitch—104 (106, 110, 114) stitches. Continue until Sleeve measures 17½ (18, 18½, 19)" (44.5 [45.5, 47, 48.5]cm) from the beginning, ending with a wrong-side row.

SHAPE SADDLE

Bind off 42 (43, 45, 47) stitches on the next row, work Chart G as established, work to the end of the row.

NEXT ROW Bind off 42 (43, 45, 47) stitches, work to the end of the row—20 stitches remain for the saddle. Work even on the saddle stitches, keeping continuity of Chart G, with one reverse stockinette stitch on each side of Chart G, until the saddle measures approximately 6¾ (7½, 8, 8½)" (17 [19, 20.5, 21.5]cm) in length, ending with a wrong-side row. Bind off all stitches, decreasing 5 stitches evenly by k2tog or p2tog accordingly across Chart G during the bind off.

finishing

Sew the long edges of the saddles along the shoulders of Front and Back. Sew the bound-off edges of Sleeves along the side edges of Front and Back. Sew side and sleeve seams.

NECKBAND

With smaller circular needle and right side facing, pick up and knit 100 (100, 105, 105) stitches evenly around the neck edge beginning at left side of Back. Place a marker for the beginning of round and join. Work the 5-stitch repeat of Chart A for 2" (5cm). Bind off loosely in pattern.

Weave in all loose ends and block gently to measurements.

chart a   chart b

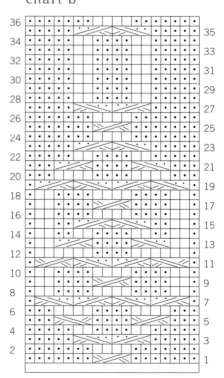

key on
page 113

5-Stitch Repeat

18 Stitches

Handspun Romney/Border Leicester crossbred and mohair, hand dyed

chart c

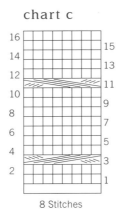

8 Stitches

chart d

48 Stitches

chart e

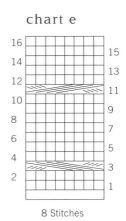

8 Stitches

chart f

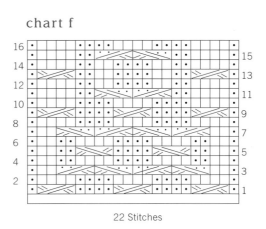

22 Stitches

chart g

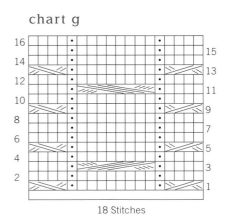

18 Stitches

key

☐ = K on RS, p on WS

• = P on RS, k on WS

= Slip next st onto cn and hold in back, k1, k1 from cn

= Slip next st onto cn and hold in front, k1, k1 from cn

= Slip 2 sts onto cn and hold in back, k2, k2 from cn

= Slip 2 sts onto cn and hold in front, k2, k2 from cn

= Slip 2 sts onto cn and hold in back, k2, p2 from cn

= Slip 2 sts onto cn and hold in front, p2, k2 from cn

= Slip 4 sts onto cn and hold in back, k4, k4 from cn

= Slip 4 sts onto cn and hold in front, k4, k4 from cn

staghorn

Staghorn was born as an adult-sized version of a baby's Aran I designed several years ago. Thinking I could simply upsize the design only by changing gauge proved to be a mistake. After weeks manipulating the cable motifs, I stumbled upon the arrangement you see here. The earthy handspun version is wool that resulted from a happy accidental crossbreeding that created incredibly beautiful wool in both color and texture that I have failed to find again. Green Mountain Spinnery's Mountain Mohair is consistently a yarn that rises to any occasion I present to it. The color reminds me of partridgeberry leaves encountered on a forest floor.

SKILL LEVEL ○ ○ ○
Experienced

FINISHED MEASUREMENTS
CHEST 40 (44, 48, 52)" (101.5 [112, 122, 132]cm)
LENGTH 25 (27, 27, 27)" (63.5 [68.5, 68.5, 68.5]cm)
Note Finished Length may be adjusted by working more or less repeats of Chart C. Each 16-row repeat of Chart C is approximately 2" (5cm). Please allow extra yardage for longer length.

YARN medium
1,350 (1,500, 1,650, 1,800) yds (1,234 [1,372, 1,509, 1,646]m) heavy worsted weight
MODEL AT LEFT Handspun Karakul/ Corriedale/Coopworth crossbred (100%), natural light brown

MODEL AT RIGHT 10 (11, 12, 13) skeins Green Mountain Spinnery Mountain Mohair, 2 oz (56g) skeins, each approximately 140 yds (128m), 30% mohair, 70% wool, Elderberry

NEEDLES & NOTIONS
US size 5 (3.75mm) knitting needles
US size 7 (4.5mm) knitting needles, or size needed to obtain gauge
US size 5 (3.75mm) circular needle, 16" (40cm) long
Cable needle
Stitch markers
Tapestry needle

GAUGE
16 stitches and 28 rows = 4" (10cm) over double moss stitch using larger needles. Adjust needle size as necessary to obtain correct gauge.

P2, K2 RIBBING
ROW 1 (RS) (P2, k2) across
ROW 2 (WS) (K2, p2) across
Repeat these two rows for pattern.

P1, K2 RIBBING
ROW 1 (RS) (P1, k2) across
ROW 2 (WS) (P2, k1) across
Repeat these two rows for pattern.

DOUBLE MOSS STITCH
ROWS 1 AND 2 (P2, k2) across.
ROWS 3 AND 4 (K2, p2) across.
Repeat these 4 rows for pattern.

left Handspun Karakul/Corriedale/Coopworth crossbred right Green Mountain Spinnery Mountain Mohair

staghorn

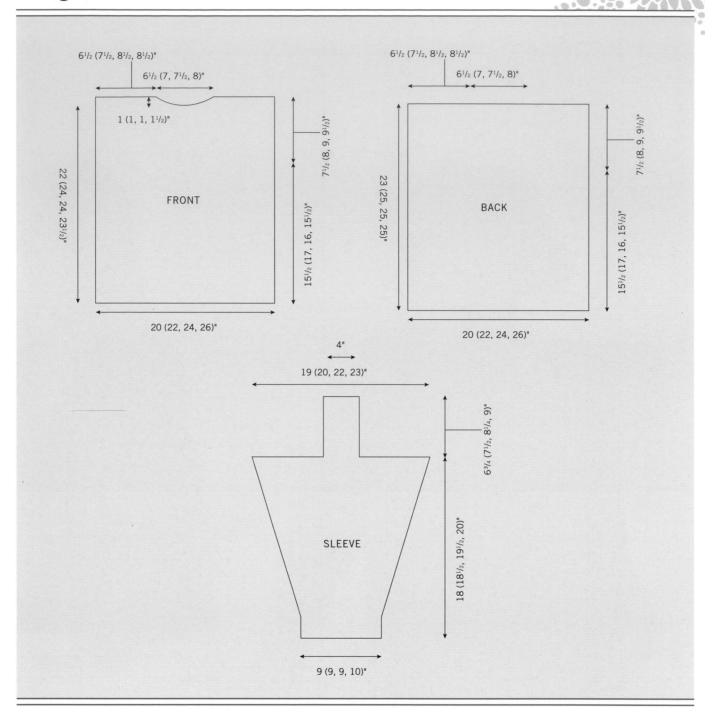

6½ (7½, 8½, 8½)"

6½ (7, 7½, 8)"

1 (1, 1, 1½)"

FRONT

22 (24, 24, 23½)"

20 (22, 24, 26)"

7½ (8, 9, 9½)"

15½ (17, 16, 15½)"

6½ (7½, 8½, 8½)"

6½ (7, 7½, 8)"

BACK

23 (25, 25, 25)"

20 (22, 24, 26)"

7½ (8, 9, 9½)"

15½ (17, 16, 15½)"

4"

19 (20, 22, 23)"

SLEEVE

6¾ (7½, 8¼, 9)"

18 (18½, 19½, 20)"

9 (9, 9, 10)"

back

With smaller needles, cast on 112 (120, 128, 136) stitches.

RIBBING SETUP ROW Work p2, k2 rib over 30 (34, 38, 42) stitches, ending with p2, work Chart B over 12 stitches, work p1, k2 rib over 28 stitches, ending with p1, work Chart B over 12 stitches, work p2, k2 rib over 30 (34, 38, 42) stitches, ending with p2. Continue working ribbing pattern and Chart B until the piece measures approximately 3" (7.5cm) from the beginning, ending with row 4 of Chart B.

Main Body Pattern

ROW 1 (RS) Change to larger needles. Work double moss stitch over 8 (12, 16, 20) stitches, work Chart A over 22 stitches, work Chart B as established over 12 stitches, work Chart C over 28 stitches, work Chart B over 12 stitches as established, work Chart A over 22 stitches, work double moss stitch over 8 (12, 16, 20) stitches. Continue working all Charts until the piece measures approximately 23 (25, 25, 25)" (58.5 [63.5, 63.5, 63.5]cm) from the beginning, ending with row 8 or 16 of Chart C. Bind off all stitches.

front

Work as for Back until the piece measures 22 (24, 24, 23½)" (56 [61, 61, 59.5]cm) from beginning, or 1 (1, 1, 1½)" (2.5 [2.5, 2.5, 3.8]cm) less than Back.

SHAPE FRONT NECK

Keeping continuity of all Charts, work across 39 (42, 44, 48) stitches for shoulder, join second ball of yarn, bind off center 34 (36, 40, 40) stitches for front neck, work across remaining 39 (42, 44, 48) stitches for the second shoulder. Using two balls of yarn and working both sides at the same time, decrease 1 stitch at each neck edge every right-side row 3 (3, 3, 4) times as follows: Work across first shoulder until 3 stitches remain, k2tog, k1 (for neck selvedge). For second shoulder, k1 (for neck selvedge), ssk, work to end—36 (39, 41, 44) stitches remain for each shoulder. Work even until Front measures same length as Back. Bind off shoulder stitches.

sleeves (MAKE 2)

With smaller needles, cast on 54 (54, 54, 58) stitches.

Ribbing Setup Row

SIZES 40, 44, AND 48 ONLY K2, p2, work Chart B over 12 stitches, work p2, k2 rib over 22 stitches, ending with p2, work Chart B over 12 stitches, p2, k2

SIZE 52 ONLY P2, k2, p2, work Chart B over 12 stitches, work p2, k2 rib over 22 stitches, ending with p2, work Chart B over 12 stitches, p2, k2, p2.

ALL SIZES Continue until the piece measures approximately 3" (7.5cm) from the beginning, ending with row 4 of Chart B.

Main Sleeve Pattern

SIZES 40, 44, AND 48 ONLY Change to larger needles. P1, k2, place marker (pm), p1, work Chart B as established over 12 stitches, work Chart A over center 22 stitches, work Chart B as established over 12 stitches, p1, pm, k2, p1.

SIZE 52 ONLY Change to larger needles. P2, k2, p1, place marker (pm), p1, work Chart B as established over 12 stitches, work Chart A over center 22 stitches, work Chart B as established over 12 stitches, p1, pm, p1, k2, p2.

ALL SIZES Continue working all Charts, increasing 1 stitch at each edge every 4 rows 4 (9, 17, 15) times, then every 6 rows 14 (11, 7, 9) times, using m1 left and right accordingly, working the new stitches into double moss stitch—90 (94, 102, 106) stitches. Work even until Sleeve measures 18 (18½, 19½, 20)" (45.5 [47, 49.5, 51]cm) ending with row 8 of Chart A.

SHAPE SADDLE

Bind off 33 (35, 39, 41) stitches at the beginning of the next 2 rows. Continue working Chart A as established over remaining 24 stitches with 1 stockinette stitch on each side for selvedge stitches, until the saddle measures 6¾ (7½, 8¼, 9)" (17 [18.5, 21, 23]cm) in length, ending with row 8 of Chart A. Bind off remaining stitches.

finishing

Sew the long edges of the saddles along the shoulders of Fronts and Back. Sew the bound-off edges of Sleeves along the side edges of Fronts and Back. Sew side and sleeve seams.

NECKBAND

With smaller circular needle and right side facing, pick up and knit 72 (76, 78, 88) stitches evenly around the neck edge beginning at the left shoulder. Work in k2, p2 rib until the neckband measures 1" (2.5cm). Bind off loosely.

Weave in all loose ends and block gently to measurements.

chart a

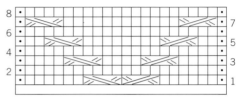

22 Stitches

chart b

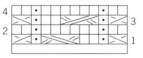

12 Stitches

chart c

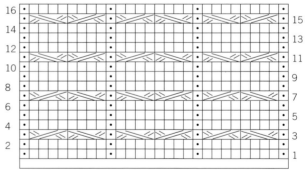

28 Stitches

key

☐ = K on RS, p on WS

• = P on RS, k on WS

⧖ = Slip next st onto cn and hold in back, k1, k1 from cn

⧖ = Slip next st onto cn and hold in front, k1, k1 from cn

⧖ = Slip 2 sts onto cn and hold in back, k2, k2 from cn

⧖ = Slip 2 sts onto cn and hold in front, k2, k2 from cn

ruby

This little vest is simply a vehicle for a wool blend designed to replicate the sparkle of rubies. The name just sounded good as one half of a twinset: Ruby & Harriet (page 124).

For a few years now, I've been smitten with Barbara Parry's spinning blends featuring Angelina® fiber, also used in Twilight (page 64). The metal fiber is like delicate Christmas tinsel, and Barb's quiet use of it mingled with her extraordinary colors delights me endlessly. Watching the glint of it in the sun on a whirring bobbin gives hints of the beauty of the garment waiting to be knit from it. It occurred to me that the sparkle emitted from the shadows of the wool is very gemlike, with the Angelina revealing itself only upon the movement of the fiber or the resulting yarn. I chose Ruby as the theme for the fiber because I adore any shade of red and because Ruby doubles as an old-fashioned and ladylike name that added to the elements of the twinset's design.

I chose two shades of red to dye the white wool from Barb's Border Leicester sheep named Amethyst. (It's pure and serendipitous happenstance that the sheep played a direct role in my conceptual design!) A rich turkey red and a dark and brooding cranberry are melded together to make this lustrous ruby red yarn. I chose a fuchsia Angelina fiber to blend instead of the obvious red to allow it to stand out a bit. I love their color properties, and although I wish I had added more Angelina to the final blend, the faint sparkle is very demure, which fits in with the ladylike theme.

The bronze alpaca yarn gives a completely different mood to the vest although both models feature fibers with subtle halos, and both exhibit extraordinary softness. The simple eyelet pattern is like opening a jewelry box and seeing a sparkling gem inside.

front Handspun Border Leicester with Angelina®, hand dyed back Frog Tree Yarns Alpaca Sport

ruby

SKILL LEVEL ● ● ○
Intermediate

FINISHED
MEASUREMENTS
CHEST 37½ (40, 42, 45½, 48,
50)" (95 [101.5, 106.5, 115.5,
122, 127]cm)
LENGTH 18½ (20, 20½, 21½, 22,
22½)" (47 [51, 52, 54.5, 56,
57]cm)

YARN 🔲 fine
750 (850, 950, 1,050, 1,150,
1,250) yds (686 [777, 869, 960,
1,052, 1,143]m) sport weight
MODEL AT FRONT Handspun
Border Leicester (100%) with
Angelina®, hand dyed ruby red
MODEL AT BACK 6 (7, 8, 9, 9, 10)
skeins Frog Tree Yarns Alpaca
Sport, 1¾ oz (50g) skeins, each
approximately 130 yds (119m),
100% alpaca, 13 Bronze

NEEDLES & NOTIONS
US size 2 (2.75mm) knitting
   needles
US size 3 (3.25mm) knitting
   needles, or size needed to
   obtain gauge
US size 2 (2.75mm) circular
   needle, 24" (60cm) long
US size 2 (2.75mm) circular
   needle, 29" (74cm) long
Stitch holders
Stitch markers
Tapestry needle
5 buttons, ⅝" (1.6cm) in diameter

GAUGE
24 stitches and 32 rows = 4"
(10cm) over Chart A or B with
larger needles. Adjust needle size
as necessary to obtain correct
gauge.

NOTE
The first and last stitch of every
row is worked in stockinette
stitch for a selvedge stitch at the
front edges.

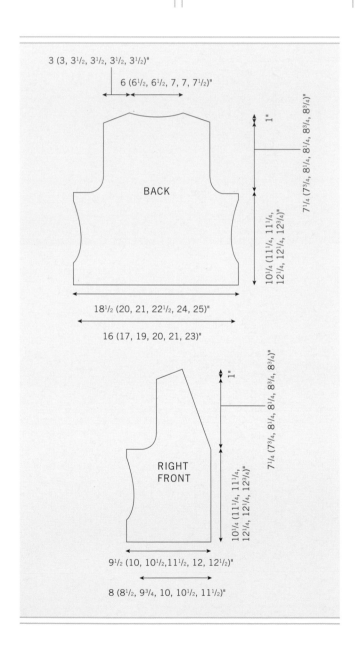

back

With smaller needles, cast on 111 (119, 127, 135, 143, 151) stitches.
Ribbing Pattern
NOTE The stitch count does not remain constant and changes every row.
ROW 1 (RS) K1 (selvedge stitch), p1, *slip 1, k2, psso, p2, k1, p2;
repeat from *, end slip 1, k2, psso, p1, k1 (selvedge stitch).
ROW 2 P1, k1, *p1, yo, p1, k2, p1, k2; repeat from *, end p1, yo,
p1, k1, p1.
ROW 3 K1, p1, *k3, p2, k1, p2; repeat from *, end k3, p1, k1.
ROW 4 P1, k1, *p3, k2, p1, k2; repeat from *, end p3, k1, p1.
Continue until piece measures 2½" (6.5cm), ending with row 4 of
ribbing pattern.
Main Body Pattern
ROW 1 (RS) Change to larger needles. K1 (selvedge stitch), work Chart A
over 109 (117, 125, 133, 141, 149) stitches, k1 (selvedge stitch).
Continue working Chart A and *at the same time*, shape waist, beginning
with the next right-side row.

SHAPE WAIST
DECREASE ROW (RS) K1 (selvedge stitch), ssk, knit across to last 3
stitches, k2tog, k1 (selvedge stitch).
Repeat Decrease Row on right-side rows every 4 (2, 4, 4, 4, 6) rows 6
(0, 0, 2, 4, 4) more times, then every 0 (4, 6, 6, 6, 8) rows 0 (7, 5, 4, 3,
1) times—97 (103, 115, 121, 127, 139) stitches, ending with a wrong-
side row.
INCREASE ROW (RS) K1 (selvedge stitch), m1 right, knit across the row
until one stitch remains, m1 left, k1 (selvedge stitch). Repeat Increase
Row on right-side rows every 0 (4, 6, 6, 6, 8) rows 0 (6, 4, 3, 2, 0)
more times, then every 4 (2, 4, 4, 4, 6) rows 7 (1, 1, 3, 5, 5) times—
111 (119, 127, 135, 143, 151) stitches.
Continue until Back measures 10¼ (11¼, 11¼, 12¼, 12¼, 12¾)" (26
[28.5, 28.5, 31, 31, 32.5]cm) from the beginning, ending with a wrong-
side row.

SHAPE ARMHOLE

Bind off 9 (11, 12, 13, 14, 16) stitches at the beginning of the next 2 rows.

DECREASE ROW (RS) K1 (selvedge stitch), ssk, work across to last 3 stitches, k2tog, k1 (selvedge stitch). Continue to work Decrease Row every other row 8 (9, 10, 11, 13, 14) more times—75 (77, 81, 85, 87, 89) stitches. Work even until the armhole measures 7¼ (7¾, 8¼, 8¼, 8¾, 8¾)" (18.5 [19.5, 21, 21, 22, 22]cm), ending with row 6 or 12 of Chart A.

SHAPE SHOULDERS AND BACK NECK

ROWS 1 AND 2 Bind off 7 (7, 7, 7, 8, 8) stitches at the beginning of each row.

ROW 3 Bind off 6 (6, 7, 7, 7, 7) stitches, work 10 (10, 11, 11, 11, 11) stitches, join a second ball of yarn and bind off center 35 (37, 38, 42, 42, 44) stitches for back neck, work to the end of the row.

ROW 4 Using two balls of yarn and working both sides at the same time, bind off 6 (6, 6, 6, 6, 6) stitches at the beginning of the row, work to end, work across second shoulder stitches.

ROW 5 Bind off 6 (6, 7, 7, 7, 7) stitches at the beginning of the row, decrease 1 stitch at each neck edge as follows: work until 3 stitches remain for first shoulder, k2tog, k1 (selvedge). For second shoulder, k1 (for neck selvedge), ssk, work to end.

ROW 6 Bind off 6 (6, 7, 7, 7, 7) stitches.

right front

With smaller needles, cast on 56 (60, 64, 68, 72, 76) stitches.

Ribbing Pattern

NOTE The stitch count does not remain constant and changes every row.

For Sizes 37½, 42, and 48 Only

ROW 1 (RS) K1 (selvedge stitch), k1, p2, k1, p2, *slip 1, k2, psso, p2, k1, p2; repeat from *, end k1 (selvedge stitch).

ROW 2 P1, k2, p1, k2, *p1, yo, p1, k2, p1, k2; repeat from *, end p2.

ROW 3 K2, p2, k1, p2, *k3, p2, k1, p2; repeat from *, end k1.

ROW 4 P1, k2, p1, k2, *p3, k2, p1, k2; repeat from *, end p2.

For Sizes 40, 45½, and 50 Only

ROW 1 K1 (selvedge stitch), p2, *slip 1, k2, psso, p2, k1, p2; repeat from *, end k1 (selvedge stitch).

ROW 2 P1, k2, p1, k2, *p1, yo, p1, k2, p1, k2; repeat from *, end p1, yo, p1, k2, p1.

ROW 3 K1, p2, *k3, p2, k1, p2; repeat from *, end k1.

ROW 4 P1, k2, p1, k2, *p3, k2, p1, k2; repeat from *, end p1, yo, p1, k2, p1.

All Sizes

Continue until the piece measures 2½" (6.5cm), ending with row 4 of ribbing pattern.

Main Body Pattern

ROW 1 (RS) Change to larger needles. K1 (selvedge stitch), k1, beginning with stitch 1 (5, 1, 5, 1, 5) of the 8-stitch repeat, work Chart B over 53 (57, 61, 65, 69, 73) stitches, end k1 (selvedge stitch). Continue working Chart B and *at the same time*, shape waist beginning with the next right-side row.

Frog Tree Yarns Alpaca Sport

DECREASE ROW (RS) K1 (selvedge stitch), work as established to last 3 stitches, k2tog, k1 (selvedge stitch).

Repeat Decrease Row every 4 (2, 4, 4, 4, 6) rows 6 (0, 0, 2, 4, 4) more times, then every 0 (4, 6, 6, 6, 8) rows 0 (7, 5, 4, 3, 1) times—49 (52, 58, 61, 64, 70) stitches, ending with a wrong-side row.

INCREASE ROW (RS) K1 (selvedge stitch), work across until one stitch remains, m1 left, k1 (selvedge stitch).

Repeat Increase Row every 0 (4, 6, 6, 6, 8) rows 0 (6, 4, 3, 2, 0) more times, then every 4 (2, 4, 4, 4, 6) rows 7 (1, 1, 3, 5, 5) times—56 (60, 64, 68, 72, 76) stitches.

Continue until Right Front measures 10¼ (11¼, 11¼, 12¼, 12¼, 12¾)" (26 [28.5, 28.5, 31, 31, 32.5]cm) from the beginning, ending with a right-side row.

SHAPE ARMHOLE AND V-NECK

Bind off 9 (11, 12, 13, 14, 16) stitches at the beginning of the next wrong-side row for armhole.

NEXT ROW (RS) K1, ssk, work as established to last 3 stitches, k2tog, k1.

Continue to decrease 1 stitch at the beginning of every right-side row using ssk 9 (10, 8, 10, 10, 10) more times, then every fourth right-side row 9 (9, 11, 11, 11, 12) times for neck.

At the same time, decrease 1 stitch at the end of every right-side row using k2tog 8 (9, 10, 11, 13, 14) more times for armhole—19 (19, 21, 21, 22, 22) stitches remain for shoulder.

Work even until the armhole measures 7¼ (7¾, 8¼, 8¼, 8¾, 8¾)" (18.5 [19.5, 21, 21, 22, 22]cm), or same length as Back to shoulders, ending with row 6 or 12 of Chart B.

Frog Tree Yarns Alpaca Sport

SHAPE SHOULDER
ROWS 1, 3, AND 5 (RS) Work even.
ROW 2 Bind off 7 (7, 7, 7, 8, 8) stitches at the beginning of the row.
ROW 4 Bind off 6 (6, 7, 7, 7, 7) stitches at the beginning of the row.
ROW 6 Bind off 6 (6, 7, 7, 7, 7) stitches.

left front
With smaller needle, cast on 56 (60, 64, 68, 72, 76) stitches.
Ribbing Pattern
NOTE The stitch count does not remain constant and changes every row.

For Sizes 37½, 42, and 48 Only
ROW 1 K1 (selvedge stitch), p2, k1, p2, *slip 1 k 2, psso, p2, k1, p2 * repeat from *, end, k1, k1 (selvedge stitch).
ROW 2 P2, k2, p1, k2, *p1, yo, p1, k2, p1, k2 * repeat from *, end p1.
ROW 3 K1, p2, k1, p2, *k3, p2, k1, p2 * repeat from *, end k1, k1.
ROW 4 P2, k2, p1, k2, *p3, k2, p1, k2* repeat from *, end p1.
For Sizes 40, 45½, and 50 Only
ROW 1 K1 (selvedge stitch), p2, k1, p2, *slip 1, k2, psso, p2, k1, p2; repeat from *, end slip 1, k2, psso, p2, k1 (selvedge stitch).
ROW 2 P1, k2, *p1, yo, p1, k2, p1, k2; repeat from *, end p1.
ROW 3 K1, p2, k1, p2, *k3, p2, k1, p2; repeat from *, end k3, p2, k1.
ROW 4 P1, k2, *p3, k2, p1, k2; repeat from *, end p1.
All Sizes
Continue until the piece measures 2½" (6.5cm), ending with row 4 of ribbing pattern.

Main Body Pattern

ROW 1 (RS) Change to larger needles. K1 (selvedge stitch), work the 8-stitch repeat of Chart B over 53 (57, 61, 65, 69, 73) stitches ending with stitch 13 (8, 13, 8, 13, 8), end k1, k1 (selvedge stitch).

Continue working Chart B and *at the same time*, shape waist beginning with the next right-side row.

DECREASE ROW (RS) K1 (selvedge stitch), ssk, work as established across row.

Repeat Decrease Row every 4 (2, 4, 4, 4, 6) rows 6 (0, 0, 2, 4, 4) more times, then every 0 (4, 6, 6, 6, 8) rows 0 (7, 5, 4, 3, 1) times—49 (52, 58, 61, 64, 70) stitches, ending with a wrong-side row.

INCREASE ROW (RS) K1 (selvedge stitch), m1 right, work as established across row.

Repeat Increase Row every 0 (4, 6, 6, 6, 8) rows 0 (6, 4, 3, 2, 0) more times, then every 4 (2, 4, 4, 4, 6) rows 7 (1, 1, 3, 5, 5) times—56 (60, 64, 68, 72, 76) stitches.

Continue until Left Front measures 10¼ (11¼, 11¼, 12¼, 12¼, 12¾)" (26 [28.5, 28.5, 31, 31, 32.5]cm) from the beginning, ending with a wrong-side row.

SHAPE ARMHOLE AND V-NECK

Bind off 9 (11, 12, 13, 14, 16) stitches at the beginning of the next right-side row for armhole.

NEXT ROW (RS) K1, ssk, work as established to last 3 stitches, k2tog, k1.

Continue to decrease 1 stitch at the end of every right-side row using k2tog 9 (10, 8, 10, 10, 10) more times, then every fourth right-side row 9 (9, 11, 11, 11, 12) times for neck. *At the same time*, decrease one stitch at the beginning of every right-side row using ssk 8 (9, 10, 11, 13, 14) more times for armhole—19 (19, 21, 21, 22, 22) stitches remain for shoulder.

Work even until the armhole measures 7¼ (7¾, 8¼, 8¼, 8¾, 8¾)" (18.5 [19.5, 21, 21, 22, 22]cm), or same length as Back to shoulders, ending with row 5 or 11 of Chart B.

SHAPE SHOULDERS

ROWS 1 (RS) Bind off 7 (7, 7, 7, 8, 8) stitches at the beginning of the row.

ROWS 2, 4, AND 6 Work even.

ROW 3 Bind off 6 (6, 7, 7, 7, 7) stitches at the beginning of the row.

ROW 5 Bind off 6 (6, 7, 7, 7, 7) stitches.

finishing

Sew shoulder and side seams.

ARMHOLE EDGING

With 24" (60cm) circular needle and right side facing, pick up and knit 112 (126, 133, 133, 140, 147) stitches evenly around armhole beginning at the underarm. Place marker for the beginning of round.

RIBBING PATTERN *K2, p2, k1, p2; repeat from * around. Work until the edging measures 1" (2.5cm). Bind off loosely in pattern. Repeat for the second armhole.

FRONT BANDS

With 29" (74cm) circular needle and right side facing, begin at the lower right edge, pick up and knit 74 (74, 80, 85, 86, 86) stitches along the right front edge to the first neck decrease, place marker, pick up and knit 49 (52, 56, 56, 59, 59) stitches along the right side of the V-neck edge, 43 (44, 45, 49, 48, 48) stitches along the back neck, 49 (52, 56, 56, 59, 59) stitches along the left side of the V-neck edge, place marker, pick up and knit 74 (74, 80, 85, 86, 86) stitches along the left front edge—289 (296, 317, 331, 338, 338) stitches.

RIBBING PATTERN (WS) * P2, k2, p1, k2; repeat from *, end p2.

NEXT ROW Knit the knit stitches and purl the purl stitches as they appear.

Work one more row.

BUTTONHOLE ROW (RS) Work 8 (8, 7, 8, 8, 8) stitches, *bind off 2 stitches, work 13 (13, 15, 16, 16, 16) stitches; repeat from * 3 more times, bind off 2 stitches, end k4 (4, 3, 3, 4, 4) stitches before marker, work to the end of row.

NEXT ROW (WS) Work across row in established ribbing, casting on 2 stitches over bound-off stitches. Work 2 more rows then bind off loosely in pattern on the right side.

Sew buttons opposite buttonholes. Weave in all loose ends. Hand wash and block gently to measurements.

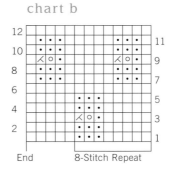

chart a

chart b

key

☐ = K on RS, p on WS

· = P on RS, k on WS

⋌ = P2tog

○ = Yarn over (yo)

harriet

Shetland knitting fascinates me, and I enjoy placing basic Shetland stitches in garments in such a way that lends their delicate air but does not complicate the knitting itself. This cardigan features two traditional stitches worked in separate areas and placed so that the shaping doesn't interfere very much with the lace patterns. A wide band at the lower edge features the classic razor shell pattern, which provides a feminine scalloped edge. The lace panels on the body are openwork versions of cables. The yarns used are DK weight but I chose to work them at a softened gauge to allow the lace to open up.

The handspun version features pure Shetland wool from a sheep named Harriet, and the sheep did indeed inspire the name and the garment itself. The commercial model's yarn is a close comparison to the handspun. Even though the commercial yarn is not made from pure Shetland wool, it is Scottish and the fabrics knitted from the two yarns are very similar.

SKILL LEVEL ○ ○ ○
Intermediate Beginner

FINISHED MEASUREMENTS
CHEST 41 (45, 49, 53)" (104 [114, 124.5, 134.5]cm)
LENGTH 23½ (23½, 26½, 26½)" (59.5 [59.5, 67.5, 67.5]cm)
Note The finished length can be adjusted by 3" (7.5cm) by working more or less repeats of Chart B. Please allow extra yardage for additional length.

YARN (4) medium
1,200 (1,300, 1,500, 1,600) yds (1,097 [1,189, 1,372, 1,463]m) DK to worsted weight
MODEL AT LEFT Handspun Shetland (100%), natural black
MODEL AT RIGHT 10 (11, 12, 13) skeins Rowan Yarns Scottish Tweed DK, 1¾ oz (50g) skeins, each approximately 123 yds (113m), 100% pure new wool, 018 Thatch

NEEDLES & NOTIONS
US size 6 (4mm) knitting needles, or size needed to obtain gauge
US size 6 (4mm) circular needles, 16" (40cm) and 29" (74cm) long
Stitch holders
Tapestry needle
7 buttons, ¾" (2cm) in diameter

GAUGE
16 stitches and 24 rows = 4" (10cm) over stockinette stitch. Adjust needle size as necessary to obtain correct gauge.

left Handspun Shetland right Rowan Yarns Scottish Tweed DK

harriet

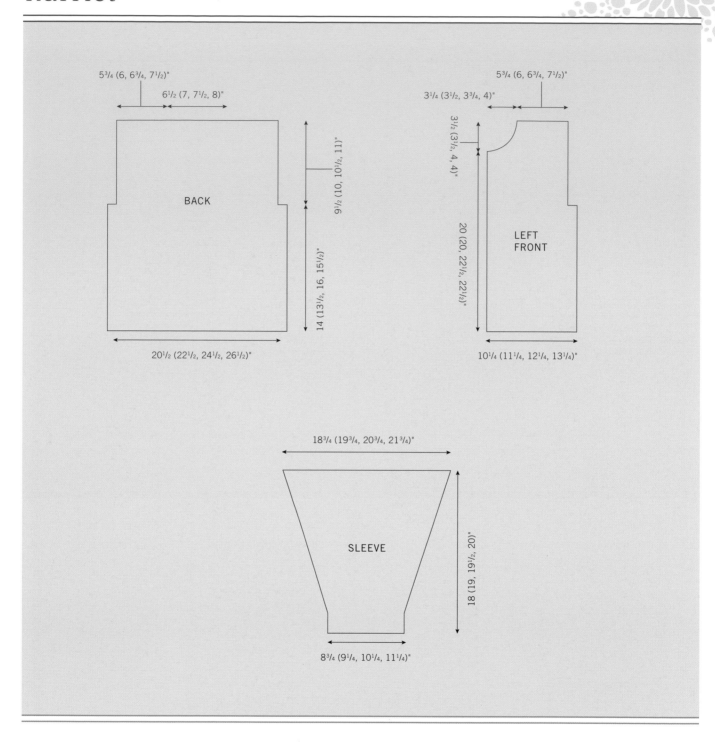

BACK

5³/₄ (6, 6³/₄, 7¹/₂)"

6¹/₂ (7, 7¹/₂, 8)"

9¹/₂ (10, 10¹/₂, 11)"

14 (13¹/₂, 16, 15¹/₂)"

20¹/₂ (22¹/₂, 24¹/₂, 26¹/₂)"

LEFT FRONT

5³/₄ (6, 6³/₄, 7¹/₂)"

3¹/₄ (3¹/₂, 3³/₄, 4)"

3¹/₂ (3¹/₂, 4, 4)"

20 (20, 22¹/₂, 22¹/₂)"

10¹/₄ (11¹/₄, 12¹/₄, 13¹/₄)"

SLEEVE

18³/₄ (19³/₄, 20³/₄, 21³/₄)"

18 (19, 19¹/₂, 20)"

8³/₄ (9¹/₄, 10¹/₄, 11¹/₄)"

back

Cast on 83 (91, 99, 107) stitches. Work in garter stitch for 4 rows (2 ridges on the right side). Keeping the first and last stitches of every row in stockinette stitch for selvedge stitches, work Chart A for 5" (12.5cm), ending with a wrong-side row, increasing 1 stitch on the last row using the m1 method—84 (92, 100, 108) stitches.

Eyelet Ridge

Work 4 rows in garter stitch.

EYELET ROW (RS) K1 (selvedge stitch), k2, *yo, k2tog; repeat from *, end k2, k1 (selvedge stitch).

Work 3 rows in garter stitch, decreasing 2 stitches evenly on the last row using k2tog—82 (90, 98, 106) stitches.

Main Body Pattern

SETUP ROW (RS) Work stockinette stitch over 8 (12, 16, 20) stitches, work Chart B over 29 stitches, work stockinette stitch over center 8 stitches, work Chart B over 29 stitches, work stockinette stitch over 8 (12, 16, 20) stitches.

Continue working as established until the piece measures 14 (13½, 16, 15½)" (35.5 [34.5, 40.5, 39.5]cm) from the beginning, ending with a wrong-side row.

SHAPE ARMHOLE

Bind off 5 (7, 7, 7) stitches at the beginning of the next two rows for armhole—72 (76, 84, 92) stitches.

Continue until the armhole measures 9½ (10, 10½, 11)" (24 [25.5, 26.5, 28]cm), ending with Row 18 of Chart B. Place remaining stitches on a holder.

left front

Cast on 43 (43, 51, 51) stitches. Work in garter stitch for 4 rows (2 ridges on right side). Keeping the first and last stitches of every row in stockinette stitch for selvedge stitches, work Chart A for 5" (12.5cm), ending with a wrong-side row, increasing 1 (5, 1, 5) stitches evenly on last row using the m1 method—44 (48, 52, 56) stitches.

Eyelet Ridge

Work 4 rows in garter stitch.

EYELET ROW (RS) K1 (selvedge stitch), k2, *yo, k2tog; repeat from *, end k2, k1 (selvedge stitch). Work 3 rows in garter stitch, decreasing 3 stitches evenly on last row using k2tog—41 (45, 49, 53) stitches.

Main Body Pattern

SETUP ROW (RS) Work stockinette stitch over 8 (12, 16, 20) stitches, work Chart B over 29 stitches, work stockinette stitch over 4 stitches. Continue until the piece measures 14 (13½, 16, 15½)" (35.5 [34, 40.5, 39.5]cm) from the beginning, ending with a wrong-side row.

SHAPE ARMHOLE

Bind off 5 (7, 7, 7) stitches at the beginning of the next row—36 (38, 42, 46) stitches. Continue as established until the armhole measures 6 (6½, 6½, 7)" (15 [16.5, 16.5, 18]cm), ending with a right-side row.

SHAPE FRONT NECK

At neck edge, bind off 6 (7, 7, 8) stitches, work to the end of the row.

DECREASE ROW (RS) Work across to last 3 stitches, k2tog, k1 (selvedge stitch). Continue to work Decrease Row every right-side row 6 (6, 7, 7) more times—23 (24, 27, 30) stitches. Work even until Front armhole measures 9½ (10, 10½, 11)" (24 [25.5, 26.5, 28]cm), or same length as Back to shoulders. Place remaining stitches on a holder.

right front

Cast on 43 (43, 51, 51) stitches. Work in garter stitch for 4 rows (2 ridges on right side). Keeping the first and last stitches of every row in stockinette stitch for selvedge stitches, work Chart A for 5" (12.5cm), ending with a wrong-side row, increasing 1 (5, 1, 5) stitches evenly on the last row using the m1 method—44 (48, 52, 56) stitches.

Eyelet Ridge

Work 4 rows in garter stitch.

EYELET ROW (RS) K1 (selvedge stitch), k2, *yo, k2tog; repeat from *, end k2, k1 (selvedge stitch).

Work 3 rows in garter stitch, decreasing 3 stitches evenly on the last row using k2tog—41 (45, 49, 53) stitches.

Main Body Pattern

SETUP ROW (RS) Work stockinette stitch over 4 stitches, work Chart B over 29 stitches, work stockinette stitch over 8 (12, 16, 20) stitches. Continue working until the piece measures 14 (13½, 16, 15½)" (35.5 [34.5, 40.5, 39.5]cm) from the beginning, ending with a right-side row.

SHAPE ARMHOLE

Bind off 5 (7, 7, 7) stitches at the beginning of the next row—36 (38, 42, 46) stitches. Continue working until armhole measures 6 (6½, 6½, 7)" (15 [16.5, 16.5, 18]cm), ending with a wrong-side row.

SHAPE FRONT NECK

At neck edge, bind off 6 (7, 7, 8) stitches, work to the end of the row.

DECREASE ROW (RS) K1, ssk, work across row as established.

Continue to work Decrease Row every right-side row 6 (6, 7, 7) more times 23 (24, 27, 30) stitches. Work even until Front armhole measures 9½ (10, 10½, 11)" (24 [25.5, 26.5, 28]cm), or same length as Back to shoulders.

JOIN SHOULDERS

Join the shoulders using a three-needle bind-off (page 152).

sleeves (MAKE 2)

Cast on 34 (36, 40, 44) stitches.

Eyelet Ridge

Work 4 rows in garter stitch.

EYELET ROW (RS) K2, *yo, k2tog; repeat from *, end k2. Work 3 rows in garter stitch, increasing 1 stitch on last row using the m1 method—35 (37, 41, 45) stitches.

Main Sleeve Pattern

SETUP ROW (RS) Work stockinette stitch over 3 (4, 6, 8) stitches, work Chart B over center 29 stitches, work stockinette stitch over 3 (4, 6, 8) stitches.

SHAPE SLEEVE

Increase 1 stitch on each edge, using m1 left and m1 right accordingly, every 4 rows 11 (12, 11, 9) times, then every 6 rows 9 (9, 10, 12) times, working new stitches in stockinette stitch—75 (79, 83, 87) stitches. Continue until Sleeve measures 18 (19, 19½, 20)" (45.5 [48.5, 49.5, 51]cm) from the beginning, ending with row 12 (18, 4, 6) of Chart B. Bind off all stitches.

finishing

Sew Sleeves into armholes. Sew sleeve and side seams.

NECKBAND

With 16" (40cm) circular needle and right side facing, pick up and knit 68 (72, 80, 84) stitches evenly around the neck edge. Working back and forth in rows, work 3 rows in garter stitch.
EYELET ROW (RS) K2, *yo, k2tog; repeat from *, end k2.
Work 3 rows in garter stitch. Bind off loosely purlwise on the right side.

BUTTON BAND (LEFT FRONT)

With 29" (74cm) circular needle and right side facing, pick up and knit 86 (86, 94, 94) stitches along the front edge. Work in garter stitch for 7 rows. Bind off loosely purlwise on the right side.

BUTTONHOLE BAND (RIGHT FRONT)

With 29" (74cm) circular needle and right side facing, pick up and knit 86 (86, 94, 94) stitches along the front edge. Work in garter stitch for 2 rows.
BUTTONHOLE ROW Work 2 stitches, bind off the next 2 stitches, *work 9 (9, 11, 11) stitches, bind off 2 stitches; repeat from * 6 times, work the last 16 (16, 12, 12) stitches.
NEXT ROW Work across row, casting on 2 stitches over bound-off stitches. Work 3 more rows in garter stitch. Bind off loosely purlwise on the right side.

Weave in all loose ends and block gently. Sew buttons opposite buttonholes.

chart a

8-Stitch Repeat   Beg

chart b

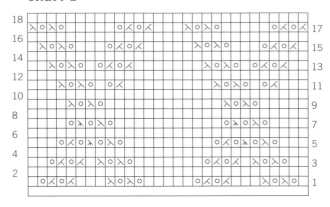

29 Stitches

key

☐ = K on RS, p on WS

◩ = K2tog

◩ = SSK

◩ = Slip 1 stitch, k2tog, pass slipped stitch over

○ = Yarn over (yo)

Rowan Yarns Scottish Tweed DK

gaelic mist

All the pieces of this design ultimately fell into place but only after hours of contemplation on just how to execute this vision of lichen and mist. Gaelic Mist began as an overengineered sweater that forced me to step back and just envision the essence of what I was trying to achieve. I took advantage of the entwining and undulating cable repeat and the organic shaping it formed at the lower edges. The soft flare at the hem is reminiscent of a peplum, and the sleeve cuffs are subtle bells. Leaving the upper body and sleeves in reverse stockinette stitch and closing off the cables make the perfect impression of the treetops disappearing into a cold mist.

The handspun Romney blended with mohair is the exact color of lichen found on trees and rocks and is the result of careful color planning. The Romney wool, from a sheep named Wisteria, is a natural gray-oatmeal. The color in the yarn contains several shades of mossy greens and lichen greens that I blended to achieve the delicate hue that I desired. This time, I was more methodical in my carding process. I blended the wool and mohair in separate batts, weighed them individually, and then blended them together, by weight, in 75% wool/25% mohair batches. Those batts were then stripped and blended twice more for homogenous color.

SKILL LEVEL ○○○
Intermediate

FINISHED MEASUREMENTS
CHEST 38 (42, 46, 50, 52½)"
(96.5 [106.5, 117, 127, 133.5]cm)
LENGTH 22 (23, 23, 24, 25)" (56
[58.5, 58.5, 61, 63.5]cm)

YARN medium
1,300 (1,400, 1,500, 1,650,
1,800) yds (1,189 [1,280, 1,372,
1,509, 1,646]m) worsted weight
MODEL AT FRONT 13 (14, 15, 16,
17) skeins Reynolds Lite Lopi, 1¾
oz (50g) skeins, each approximately
105 yds (96m), 100% Icelandic
wool, 1413 Lavender Heather

MODEL AT BACK Handspun Romney
(75%) and Mohair (25%), hand
dyed lichen green

NEEDLES & NOTIONS
US size 7 (4.5mm) knitting
   needles, or size needed to
   obtain gauge
US size 7 (4.5mm) circular
   needles, 24" (60cm) and 32"
   (81cm) long
Cable needle
Stitch holders
Stitch markers
Tapestry needle
5 buttons, ⅝" (1.6cm) in diameter

GAUGE
18 stitches and 24 rows = 4"
(10cm) in reverse stockinette

stitch. Adjust needle size as
necessary to obtain correct gauge.

**REVERSE STOCKINETTE
STITCH**
Purl all stitches on right-side
rows and knit all stitches on
wrong-side rows.

NOTE
The cardigan is worked in one
piece, back and forth in rows,
from the lower edge to the armhole.
Back and Fronts are then worked
separately and shoulders are
joined with a three-needle bind-
off. Sleeves are worked flat,
seamed, and then joined into
the body armhole.

front Reynolds Lite Lopi back Handspun Romney and mohair, hand dyed

gaelic mist

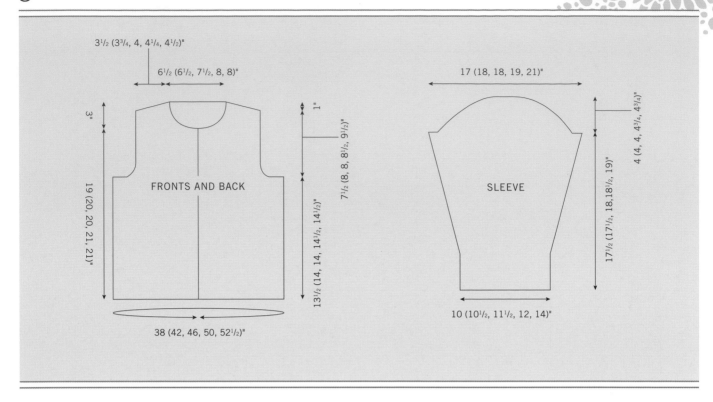

lower body

With longest circular needle, cast on 226 (250, 274, 298, 314) stitches, do not join. Working back and forth, work 4 rows in garter stitch (2 ridges on right side), ending with a wrong-side row.

Main Body Pattern

SETUP ROW (RS) K1 (selvedge stitch), p2, work Chart A, working stitches 1–6, then working the 8-stitch repeat over 208 (232, 256, 280, 296) stitches, ending with stitch 20, until 3 stitches remain, p2, k1 (selvedge stitch). Continue working Chart A, working decreases on rows 61, 63, and 65—170 (188, 206, 224, 236) stitches remain. Piece should measure approximately 10" (25.5cm) from the beginning. Continuing in reverse stockinette stitch over all stitches, keeping selvedge stitches in stockinette stitch, work even until the piece measures 13½ (14, 14, 14½, 14½)" (34.5 [35.5, 35.5, 37, 37]cm) from the beginning, ending with a wrong-side row.

upper body

DIVIDE FOR FRONT AND BACK AND SHAPE ARMHOLE

Break yarn and place the first and the last 42 (47, 51, 56, 59) stitches for Fronts onto holders—86 (94, 104, 112, 118) stitches remain for Back. Reattach yarn at Back with right side facing and bind off 6 (8, 9, 10, 11) stitches, work across Back stitches. Bind off 6 (8, 9, 10, 11) stitches at the beginning of the next row.

DECREASE ROW (WS) P1 (selvedge stitch), ssk, work across to last 3 stitches, k2tog, p1 (selvedge stitch). Continue to work Decrease Row every wrong-side row 5 (6, 7, 8, 9) more times—62 (64, 70, 74, 76) stitches remain. Work even until the armhole measures 7½ (8, 8, 8½, 9½)" (19 [20.5, 20.5, 21.5, 24]cm).

SHAPE SHOULDERS

Using short rows (page 152), shape each shoulder at side edge as follows:

ROWS 1 AND 2 Work to last 6 (6, 6, 7, 7) stitches, wrap and turn.

ROWS 3 AND 4 Work to last 11 (12, 12, 13, 14) stitches, wrap and turn.

ROWS 5 AND 6 Work across all stitches, picking up wraps.

Place 16 (17, 18, 19, 20) stitches for each shoulder on holders and center 30 (30, 34, 36, 36) stitches on a holder for back neck.

right front

SHAPE ARMHOLE

Place 42 (47, 51, 56, 59) Right Front stitches onto needle. Begin with a right-side row and work across in reverse stockinette stitch. On next wrong-side row, bind off 6 (8, 9, 10, 11) stitches, work across row. Work one right-side row even.

DECREASE ROW (WS) P1 (selvedge stitch), ssk, work across row. Continue to work Decrease Row every wrong-side row 5 (6, 7, 8, 9) more times—30 (32, 34, 37, 38) stitches remain. Work even until the armhole measures 5½ (6, 6, 6, 7)" (14 [15, 15, 15, 18]cm), ending with a wrong-side row.

SHAPE FRONT NECK

On next right-side row, bind off 7 (8, 9, 9, 9) stitches.

DECREASE ROW (WS) Work as established to 3 stitches from the end, k2tog, p1 (selvedge stitch). Continue to work Decrease Row every wrong-side row 6 (6, 6, 8, 8) more times—16 (17, 18, 19, 20) stitches remain for shoulder. *At the same time*, when the armhole measures 7½ (8, 8, 8½, 9½)" (19 [20.5, 20.5, 21.5, 24]cm), begin shoulder shaping, ending with a wrong-side row.

SHAPE SHOULDERS

Using short rows (page 152), shape shoulder at side edge as follows:

ROWS 1 Work to last 6 (6, 6, 7, 7) stitches, wrap and turn.

ROWS 2 AND 4 Work to the end of the row.

ROW 3 Work to last 11 (12, 12, 13, 14) stitches, wrap and turn.

ROW 5 Work across all stitches, picking up wraps.

Place shoulder stitches on holder.

left front

SHAPE ARMHOLE

Place 42 (47, 51, 56, 59) Left Front stitches onto needle. Begin with a right-side row, bind off 6 (8, 9, 10, 11) stitches at the beginning of the row, and work across in reverse stockinette stitch.

DECREASE ROW (WS) Work across until 3 stitches remain, k2tog, p1 (selvedge stitch). Continue to work Decrease Row every wrong-side row 5 (6, 7, 8, 9) more times—30 (32, 34, 37, 38) stitches remain. Work even until the armhole measures 5½ (6, 6, 6, 7)" (14 [15, 15, 15, 18]cm), ending with a right-side row.

SHAPE FRONT NECK

On next wrong-side row, bind off 7 (8, 9, 9, 9) stitches.

DECREASE ROW (WS) P1 (selvedge stitch), ssk, work across row. Continue to work Decrease Row every wrong-side row 6 (6, 6, 8, 8) more times—16 (17, 18, 19, 20) stitches remain for shoulder. *At the same time*, when the armhole measures 7½ (8, 8, 8½, 9½)" (19 [20.5, 20.5, 21.5, 24]cm) begin shoulder shaping, ending with a wrong-side row.

SHAPE SHOULDERS

Using short rows (page 152), shape shoulder at side edge as follows:

ROWS 1, 3, AND 5 Work to the end of the row.

ROW 2 Work to last 6 (6, 6, 7, 7) stitches, wrap and turn.

ROW 4 Work to last 11 (12, 12, 13, 14) stitches, wrap and turn.

ROW 6 Work across all stitches, picking up wraps.

sleeves (MAKE 2)

Cast on 52 (54, 60, 62, 68) stitches. Work in garter stitch for 4 rows (2 ridges on right side).

Main Sleeve pattern

SETUP ROW (RS) P0 (1, 0, 1, 0), work Chart B, working stitches 1–6, then working 8-stitch repeat over 52 (52, 60, 60, 68) stitches, ending with stitches 15–20, p0 (1, 0, 1, 0).

Continue working Chart B, increasing one stitch at each edge, using m1 left and m1 right accordingly, every 8 (8, 8, 8, 6) rows 4 (4, 4, 4, 6) times, working new stitches in reverse stockinette stitch. Once Chart B is complete, there should be 46 (48, 52, 54, 62) stitches on needle. Then increase one stitch at each edge every 2 (2, 4, 4) rows 1 (5, 14, 16, 14) times, then every 4 (4, 6, 0, 6) rows 14 (12, 1, 0, 2) times— 76 (82, 82, 86, 94) stitches.

Work even until sleeve measures 17½ (17½, 18, 18½, 19)" (44.5 [44.5, 45.5, 47, 48.5]cm) from beginning, ending with a wrong-side row.

SLEEVE CAP

Bind off 4 (6, 6, 8, 5) stitches at the beginning of the next two rows.

Note Work decreases on right-side rows as follows: K1 (selvedge stitch), ssk, work across row as established to last 3 stitches, k2tog, k1 (selvedge stitch).

Work decreases on wrong-side rows as follows: P1 (selvedge stitch), p2tog, work across row as established to last 3 stitches, p2tog though the back loops, p1 (selvedge stitch).

Decrease 1 stitch at each edge every other row 4 (5, 6, 7, 5) times.

Decrease 1 stitch at each edge of every row 17 (15, 15, 13, 17) times.

Decrease 1 stitch at each edge of every other row 1 (2, 1, 2, 4) times.

Bind off 3 (3, 3, 3, 4) stitches at the beginning of the next 4 rows.

Bind off remaining 12 (14, 14, 14, 16) stitches.

finishing

Join shoulders with a three-needle bind-off (page 152). Sew sleeve seams and with right sides together, set Sleeves into armholes.

NECK AND FRONT EDGING

With 32" (81cm) circular needle and right side facing, beginning at the right lower edge, pick up and knit 98 (102, 102, 102, 108) stitches evenly along the right front edge, place marker, pick up and knit 80 (80, 80, 84, 92, 96) stitches evenly around the neck edge, place marker, pick up and knit 98 (102, 102, 102, 108) stitches evenly along the left front edge, ending at the lower left edge—276 (284, 288, 296, 312) stitches. Knit one row.

BUTTONHOLE ROW (RS) K10 (10, 10, 10, 12) stitches, bind off 2 stitches *k19 (20, 20, 20, 21) stitches, bind off 2 stitches; repeat from * 3 more times, k1, knit into the front and back of the next stitch, slip marker, knit into the front and back of the next 2 stitches, knit to 2 stitches before the second marker, knit into the front and back of the next 2 stitches, slip marker, knit into the front and back of the next stitch, knit to end.

NEXT ROW (WS) Knit across row, casting on 2 stitches over the bound-off stitches for buttonholes. Bind off loosely purlwise on the right side.

Sew buttons opposite buttonholes. Weave in all loose ends. Block flat, allowing the lower edge to ruffle slightly as desired.

Handspun Romney and mohair, hand dyed

gaelic mist

chart a

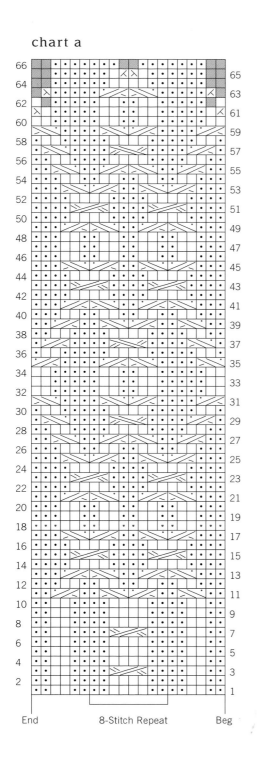

End   8-Stitch Repeat   Beg

chart b

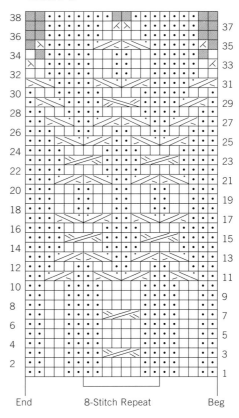

End   8-Stitch Repeat   Beg

key

- □ = K on RS, p on WS
- ⊡ = P on RS, k on WS
- ⊠ = K2tog on RS, p2tog on WS
- ⊠ = SSK on RS, p2tog through back loops on WS
- ▨ = No stitch
- = Slip next st onto cn and hold in back, k2, p1 from cn
- = Slip next 2 sts onto cn and hold in front, p1, k2 from cn
- = Slip 2 sts onto cn and hold in back, k2, k2 from cn
- = Slip 2 sts onto cn and hold in front, k2, k2 from cn

ravensong

So many artists are inspired by natural elements, and I don't feel that a clothing designer should be any different. Ravensong combines the use of color, texture, stitches, and silhouette to help me convey the essence of a raven. The charcoal Cotswold wool has a shine and character that is enchanting. This was a slightly variegated fleece, and I separated the lighter gray from the black to make a contrasting yarn for the dramatic cowl. Cotswold is sometimes called *the poor-man's mohair* because it resembles mohair in many ways. But Cotswold cannot compare to mohair, and working with this old breed of sheep's wool is a wondrous thing. The yarn changes in the varying light and truly does glisten like the plumage of a raven. I used a simple Shetland feather lace pattern and borrowed the alternating feather motif from the Ancient Oak socks for the collar.

While Cotswold wool is very dramatic, it's not really suitable for next-to-the-skin wear. However, the luscious alpaca and wool blend from Berroco can be worn this way. Both models display a beautifully subtle halo, which I think lends mystery and moodiness. The cuffs and collar can be knit using a needle three sizes larger than the needle used to knit the body, which makes the cuffs and collar dramatic and lacey, but you may choose a straighter cuff instead. Also, the loosened gauge gives a lace effect even though the weight of the handspun is closer to sport weight and the Ultra Alpaca is a worsted weight. Play with yarn and gauge to get the effect you desire for your Ravensong.

SKILL LEVEL ○ ○ ○
Intermediate Beginner

FINISHED MEASUREMENTS
CHEST 36 (39½, 43, 46, 50)" (91 [100.5, 109, 117, 127]cm)
LENGTH 21 (21, 22, 22½, 23)" (53.5 [53.5, 56, 57, 58.5]cm)

YARN 〔4〕 medium
1,000 (1,100, 1,200, 1,350, 1,450) yds (914 [1,006, 1,097, 1,234, 1,326]m) sport weight or worsted weight

MODEL AT LEFT 5 (5, 6, 7, 7) skeins Berroco Ultra Alpaca, 3½ oz (100g) skeins, each approximately 215 yds (198m), 50% superfine alpaca, 50% wool, 6282 Cranberry Mix
MODEL AT RIGHT Handspun Cotswold (100%), sport weight, natural black and gray

NEEDLES & NOTIONS
US size 8 (5mm) knitting needles, or size needed to obtain gauge
US size 11 (8mm) knitting needles (See note on Sleeves and Collar)

US size 11 (8mm) circular needle 24" (60cm) long (See note on Sleeves and Collar)
Stitch markers
Tapestry needle

GAUGE
16 stitches and 24 rows = 4" (10cm) over Chart A using smaller needles. Adjust needle size as necessary to obtain correct gauge.

NOTE
One stitch at each edge is worked in stockinette stitch for selvedge stitches throughout.

left Berroco Ultra Alpaca right Handspun Cotswold

The Raven's Song

Tell me your secrets, sweet Raven

Sing me your Song

Tell me how you slide through the sky like a shadow of night

Tell me how your eyes glisten like deep moonlight

Tell me how your feathers shine like gemstones

Tell me how your tail curves like the wind

Tell me how your wings are the story of a thousand years

Tell me how your heart beats as time

Tell me how your voice fills me with singular joy

Tell me your secrets, sweet Raven

Sing me your Song

ravensong

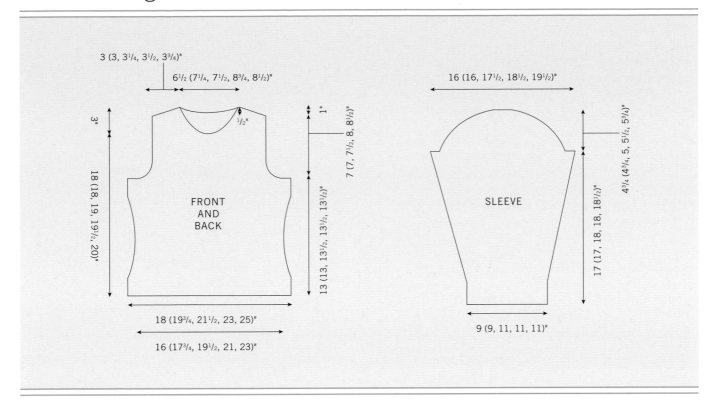

FRONT AND BACK

3 (3, 3¼, 3½, 3¾)"

6½ (7¼, 7½, 8¾, 8½)"

3"

18 (18, 19, 19½, 20)"

½"

1"

7 (7, 7½, 8, 8½)"

13 (13, 13½, 13½, 13½)"

18 (19¾, 21½, 23, 25)"

16 (17¾, 19½, 21, 23)"

SLEEVE

16 (16, 17½, 18½, 19½)"

4¾ (4¾, 5, 5½, 5¾)"

17 (17, 18, 18, 18½)"

9 (9, 11, 11, 11)"

back

With smaller needles, cast on 72 (79, 86, 93, 100) stitches. Work 4 rows in stockinette stitch, ending with a wrong-side row.

SET UP MAIN PATTERN K1 (selvedge stitch), work Chart A to last stitch, k1 (selvedge stitch). Continue working Chart A as established for 8 rows.

SHAPE WAIST

DECREASE ROW (RS) K1 (selvedge stitch), ssk, work across to last 3 stitches, k2tog, k1 (selvedge stitch).

Work Decrease Row every 8 (8, 10, 10, 10) rows 3 more times—64 (71, 78, 85, 92) stitches.

INCREASE ROW (RS) K1 (selvedge stitch), m1 right, work across row until 1 stitch remains, m1 left, k1 (selvedge stitch).

Work Increase Row every 8 (8, 10, 10, 10) rows 3 more times—72 (79, 86, 93, 100) stitches.

Continue until Back measures 13 (13, 13½, 13½, 13½)" (33 [33, 34.5, 34.5, 34.5]cm) from the beginning, ending with a wrong-side row.

SHAPE ARMHOLE

Bind off 6 (7, 8, 8, 9) stitches at the beginning of the next two rows.

DECREASE ROW (RS) K1 (selvedge stitch), ssk, work across to last 3 stitches, k2tog, k1 (selvedge stitch). Continue to work Decrease Row every other row 4 (6, 6, 6, 8) more times—50 (51, 56, 63, 64) stitches. Work even until the armhole measures 7 (7, 7½, 8, 8½)" (18 [18, 19, 20.5, 21.5]cm).

SHAPE SHOULDERS AND BACK NECK

ROW 1 Bind off 4 (4, 5, 5, 5) stitches at the beginning of the row.

ROW 2 Bind off 4 (4, 5, 5, 5) stitches at the beginning of the row, work across 8 (8, 9, 10, 10) stitches, join a second ball of yarn and bind off 24 (27, 28, 33, 32) stitches for back neck, work to the end of the row. Work both shoulders at same time with separate balls of yarn.

ROW 3 Bind off 4 (4, 4, 5, 5) stitches at the beginning of the row and decrease 1 stitch at each neck edge as follows: Work across first shoulder until 3 stitches remain, k2tog, k1 (for neck selvedge). For second shoulder, k1 (for neck selvedge), ssk, work to end.

ROW 4 Bind off 4 (4, 4, 5, 5) stitches at the beginning of the row.

ROWS 5 AND 6 Bind off 4 (3, 4, 4, 5) stitches at the beginning of each row.

front

Work as for Back until Front measures 18 (18, 19, 19½, 20)" (45.5 [45.5, 48.5, 49.5, 51]cm) from the beginning.

SHAPE FRONT NECK

Work across 19 (18, 20, 23, 24) stitches, join a second ball of yarn and bind off center 12 (15, 16, 17, 16) stitches, work to the end of the row. Decrease 1 stitch at each neck edge on every right-side row 7 (7, 7, 9, 9) times as follows: Work across first shoulder until 3 stitches remain, k2tog, k1 (for neck selvedge). For second shoulder, k1 (for neck selvedge), ssk, work to end—12 (11, 13, 14, 15) stitches remain for each shoulder. *At the same time* when armhole measures 7 (7, 7½, 8, 8½)" (18 [18, 19, 20.5, 21.5]cm), shape shoulders as for Back.

sleeves (MAKE 2)

Note A larger needle is used for a flared and lacier cuff. Choose a needle that is 3 sizes larger than the main body needle, or a needle size that makes lace that is appealing to you. For a straight sleeve, use the same size needle as used for the body for the entire sleeve.

With larger needles, cast on 37 (37, 44, 44, 44) stitches. Work 4 rows in stockinette stitch, ending with a wrong-side row.

SETUP MAIN PATTERN K1 (selvedge stitch) work Chart A to last stitch, k1 (selvedge stitch). Continue until Sleeve measures 2½" (6.5cm).

SHAPE SLEEVE

NOTE Work new stitches into chart pattern, being sure to work lace decreases only when there are enough stitches to work accompanying yarn overs within a repeat, otherwise keep new stitches at outside edges in stockinette stitch as stitches are increased. Change to smaller needle once sleeve measures 4" (10cm).

Increase one stitch at each edge, inside selvedge stitches, every 4 (4, 6, 4, 4) rows 1 (1, 8, 1, 6) times, then every 6 (6, 8, 6, 6) rows 13 (13, 5, 14, 11) times using m1 left and right accordingly—65 (65, 70, 74, 78) stitches. Work even until Sleeve measures 17 (17, 18, 18, 18½)" (43 [43, 45.5, 45.5, 47]cm) from the beginning, ending with a wrong-side row.

SLEEVE CAP

Bind off 5 (6, 7, 8, 9) stitches at the beginning of the next two rows.

NOTE Work decreases on right-side rows as follows: K1 (selvedge stitch), ssk, work across row as established to last 3 stitches, k2tog, k1 (selvedge stitch).

Work decreases on wrong-side rows as follows: P1 (selvedge stitch), p2tog, work across row as established to last 3 stitches, p2tog though the back loops, p1 (selvedge stitch).

Decrease 1 stitch at each edge every other row 5 (6, 7, 7, 8) times.
Decrease 1 stitch at each edge every row 11 (9, 7, 3, 3) times.
Decrease 1 stitch at each edge every other row 2 (2, 3, 6, 6) times.
Bind off 2 (2, 2, 3, 3) stitches at the beginning of the next 4 rows.
Bind off remaining 11 (11, 14, 14, 14) stitches.

finishing

Sew shoulder and side seams. Sew sleeve seams and with right sides together, set Sleeves into armholes.

COLLAR

With larger circular needle and wrong side facing, join yarn at right shoulder seam, pick up and knit 78 (84, 84, 90, 90) stitches evenly around neck edge, place a marker for the beginning of round. Work Chart B over all stitches. Work until collar measures 8" (20.5cm) or desired length, ending with row 10 or 20 of Chart B. Bind off very loosely.

Weave in all loose ends and block flat.

chart a

7-Stitch Repeat

chart b

6-Stitch Repeat

key

☐ = K on RS, p on WS

⊼ = K2tog

⅄ = SSK

○ = Yarn over (yo)

Handspun Cotswold

trinity

For some time, I've wanted to play with the concept of the trinity stitch and a three-strand braid. I couldn't resist placing the braid in a panel of three across the back of the vest. I employed more organic shaping, allowing the tighter gauge of the braids to form subtle shaping at the lower edge.

As a handspinner able to customize any fiber I can imagine, I took the concept of *three* even further into the fiber design. The gray handspun yarn is a careful mix of three different animal fibers: wool, alpaca, and mohair, each 33% of the total weight, in three varying shades of gray.

SKILL LEVEL
Intermediate

FINISHED MEASUREMENTS
CHEST 35 (38, 42, 45, 49)" (89 [96.5, 106.5, 114, 124.5]cm)
LENGTH 19 (19½, 20, 20½, 21)" (48.5 [49.5, 51, 52, 53.5]cm)

YARN ④ medium
600 (700, 750, 800, 850) yds (549 [640, 686, 732, 777]m) heavy worsted weight
MODEL AT FRONT Handspun Romney (33%), Mohair (33%), and Alpaca (33%), natural gray
MODEL AT BACK 3 (3, 4, 4, 4) skeins Harrisville Designs Orchid with Cashmere, 3½ oz (100g) skeins, each approximately 240 yds (220m), 25% mohair, 70% fine virgin wool, 5% cashmere, 256 Wisteria

NEEDLES & NOTIONS
US size 8 (5mm) 24" (60cm) or 32" (79cm) circular needles, or size needed to obtain gauge.
US size 8 (5mm) knitting needles, or size needed to obtain gauge.
Stitch markers
Cable needle
Stitch holders
Tapestry needle
5 buttons, ¾" (2cm) in diameter

GAUGE
18 stitches and 22 rows = 4" (10cm) in trinity stitch. Adjust needle size as necessary to obtain correct gauge.

NOTE
Vest is worked in one piece, back and forth in rows, from the lower edge to the armhole. Back and Fronts are then worked separately and shoulders are joined with a three-needle bind-off.

TRINITY STITCH
ROW 1 Purl.
ROW 2 *(K1, p1, k1) in next stitch, p3tog; rep from *.
ROW 3 Purl.
ROW 4 *P3tog, (k1, p1, k1) in next stitch; rep from *.
Repeat these 4 rows for pattern.

front Handspun Romney, Mohair, and Alpaca back Harrisville Designs Orchid with Cashmere

trinity

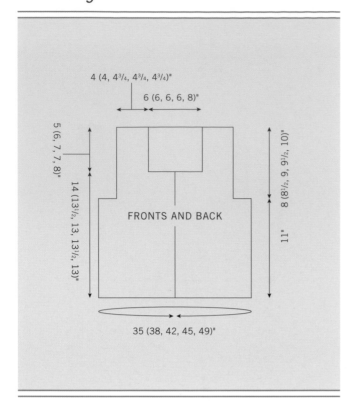

4 (4, 4¾, 4¾, 4¾)"

6 (6, 6, 6, 8)"

5 (6, 7, 7, 8)"

14 (13½, 13, 13½, 13)"

FRONTS AND BACK

8 (8½, 9, 9½, 10)"

11"

35 (38, 42, 45, 49)"

lower body

NOTE First and last stitch are worked in stockinette stitch for selvedge stitches.

With circular needle, cast on 172 (188, 204, 220, 236) stitches, do not join. Working back and forth, work 4 rows in garter stitch (2 ridges on right side), ending with a wrong-side row.

Main Body Pattern

SETUP ROW (RS) K1 (selvedge stitch), work Chart over 10 stitches, work trinity stitch over 32 (36, 40, 44, 48) stitches, place marker for side seam, work trinity stitch over 24 (28, 32, 36, 40) stitches, *work Chart over 10 stitches, work trinity stitch over 4 stitches; repeat from * once more, work Chart over 10 stitches, work trinity stitch over 24 (28, 32, 36, 40) stitches, place marker for side seam, work trinity stitch over 32 (36, 40, 44, 48) stitches, work Chart over 10 stitches, k1 (selvedge stitch). Continue until the piece measures 11" (28cm) from the beginning, or desired length to underarm.

upper body

DIVIDE FOR FRONT AND BACK AND SHAPE ARMHOLE

Break yarn and place the first and last 43 (47, 51, 55, 59) stitches onto holders for Fronts—86 (94, 102, 110, 118) stitches remain for Back. Reattach yarn at Back and bind off 11 (15, 15, 19, 19) stitches, work across row in pattern as established. Bind off 11 (15, 15, 19, 19) stitches at the beginning of the next row—64 (64, 72, 72, 80) stitches remain for Back.

Keeping 1 stitch at each edge in stockinette stitch for selvedge stitches, work even in established pattern until the armhole measures 8 (8½, 9, 9½, 10)" (20.5 [21.5, 23, 24, 25.5]cm), ending with a wrong-side row. Place all stitches on a holder.

right front

SHAPE ARMHOLE

Place 43 (47, 51, 55, 59) Right Front stitches onto the needle. With right side facing, work across in pattern. On the next wrong-side row, bind off 11 (15, 15, 19, 19) stitches, work across the row in established pattern, keeping 1 stitch at the armhole edge in stockinette stitch for a selvedge stitch—32 (32, 36, 36, 40) stitches remain.

Work until Right Front measures 14 (13½, 13, 13½, 13½)" (35.5 [34.5, 33, 34.5, 34.5]cm) from beginning, ending with a wrong-side row.

SHAPE FRONT NECK

On next right-side row, bind off 14 (14, 14, 14, 18) stitches, work across the row—18 (18, 22, 22, 22) stitches remain for shoulder. Continue in established pattern, keeping 1 stitch at the neck edge in stockinette stitch for a selvedge stitch, until the armhole measures 8 (8½, 9, 9½, 10)" (20.5 [21.5, 23, 24, 25.5]cm), or same length as Back. Place all stitches on a holder.

left front

SHAPE ARMHOLE

Place 43 (47, 51, 55, 59) Left Front stitches onto the needle. With right side facing, bind off 11 (15, 15, 19, 19) stitches at the beginning of the row, working across the row in established pattern, keeping 1 stitch at the armhole edge in stockinette stitch for a selvedge stitch—32 (32, 36, 36, 40) stitches remain. Work until Left Front measures 14 (13½, 13, 13½, 13½)" (35.5 [34.5, 33, 34.5, 34.5]cm) from the beginning, ending with a right-side row.

SHAPE FRONT NECK

On next wrong-side row, bind off 14 (14, 14, 14, 18) stitches—18 (18, 22, 22, 22) stitches remain for shoulder. Continue in established pattern, keeping one stitch at the neck edge in stockinette stitch for a selvedge stitch, until the armhole measures 8 (8½, 9, 9½, 10)" (20.5 [21.5, 23, 24, 25.5]cm), or same length as Back. Place all stitches on a holder.

finishing

Join the shoulders using a three-needle bind-off (page 152).

ARMHOLE EDGING

With right side facing and beginning at the underarm, pick up and knit 78 (80, 84, 90, 94) stitches evenly around the armhole edge. Place marker for the beginning of round and join. Work in garter stitch (purl one round, knit one round) for 4 rounds. Bind off loosely purlwise. Repeat for the second armhole.

NECK AND FRONT EDGING

With right side facing, join yarn at right lower edge, pick up and knit 62 stitches evenly along the right front edge, place marker, pick up and knit 100 (104, 120, 118, 128) stitches evenly around the neck edge, place marker, pick up and knit 62 stitches evenly along the left front edge, ending at lower edge of Left Front—224 (228, 244, 242, 252) stitches. Knit 1 row.

BUTTONHOLE ROW (RS) K2, bind off 2, *knit 12 stitches, bind off 2 stitches; repeat from * 3 more times, k1, knit into the front and back of the next stitch, slip marker, knit into the front and back of the next 2 stitches, knit to 1 stitch before the second marker, knit into the front and back of the next stitch, slip marker, knit into the front and back of the next 2 stitches, knit to end.

NEXT ROW (WS) Knit across row, casting on 2 stitches over the bound-off stitches for buttonholes.
Bind off loosely purlwise on the right side.

Sew buttons opposite buttonholes. Weave in all loose ends and block flat.

chart

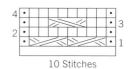

10 Stitches

key

☐ = K on RS, p on WS

· = P on RS, k on WS

= Slip 2 sts onto cn and hold in back, k2, k2 from cn

= Slip 2 sts onto cn and hold in front, k2, k2 from cn

Harrisville Designs Orchid with Cashmere

cat's eye

bottom Frog Tree Alpaca Fingering top Handspun Rambouillet Crossbred, with Angelina®

Cat's Eye is a Shetland-inspired scarf using a faux cat's eye lace pattern as opposed to the traditional Shetland stitch, which uses yarn overs on both right-side and wrong-side rows. All those yarn overs are a recipe for disaster, if you ask me, not unlike leaving your knitting available to a kitten's whims!

Sparkle and color are represented in the green handspun version with Angelina. The Frog Tree Alpaca natural white is absolutely the most perfect scarf yarn and is loved by cats far and wide.

scarf

Cast on 42 stitches and work in garter stitch for 4 rows.

FIRST BORDER

SETUP ROW K2, beginning where indicated, work Chart A across center 38 stitches, ending where indicated, k2. Continue working Chart A, keeping the first and last 2 stitches in garter stitch, until Scarf measures 2½" (6.5cm) from the beginning, ending with a wrong-side row.

Main Scarf Pattern

SETUP ROW (RS) K2, work Chart A over 11 stitches, place marker, beginning where indicated, repeat the 6-stitch repeat of Chart B over center 18 stitches, increasing 4 stitches evenly spaced using the m1 method, ending where indicated, place marker, work Chart A over 11 stitches, k2—46 stitches.

Continue until scarf measures 57½" (146cm) or 2½" (6.5cm) less than desired length, decreasing 4 stitches evenly between markers using k2tog on the last wrong-side row—42 stitches.

SECOND BORDER

SETUP ROW K2, work Chart A as for first border, ending k2, removing markers. Continue until the second border measures 2½" (6.5cm), then work garter stitch over all stitches for 4 rows. Bind off very loosely purlwise on the right side.

Weave in all loose ends and block to final measurements.

SKILL LEVEL ○○○
Intermediate Beginner

FINISHED MEASUREMENTS
Approximately 9" (23cm) x 60" (152.5cm) after blocking

YARN 2 fine
430 yds (393m) fingering weight
MODEL AT TOP Handspun Rambouillet Crossbred with Angelina® from Foxfire Fiber and Designs, Forest
MODEL AT BOTTOM 2 skeins Frog Tree Alpaca Fingering, 1¾ oz

(50g) skeins, each approximately 215 yds (197m), 100% alpaca, 000 Natural White

NEEDLES & NOTIONS
US size 6 (4mm) knitting needles, or size needed to obtain gauge.
Stitch markers
Tapestry needle

GAUGE
20 stitches = 4" (10cm) in Chart patterns. Adjust needle size as necessary to obtain correct gauge.

chart a

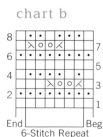

End   9-Stitch Repeat   Beg

chart b

6-Stitch Repeat

key

☐ = K on RS, p on WS

• = P on RS, k on WS

⊠ = K2tog

⊠ = SSK

⊙ = Yarn over (yo)

Stitch detail in handspun Rambouillet Crossbred with Angelina®

two hearts

With Two Hearts I set out to design a sweater of pure love. I searched for a Celtic knot to represent two hearts entwined. Once I found it and began charting it for cable knitting, I realized the knot was the familiar Saxon braid. Wanting to make the cable my own, I played a bit and devised a way to entwine the two hearts into a double motif, thereby making the love bond completely inseparable. The more I look at these cables, the more hearts I find. The loose braid resembles an abstract heart and within the basic element of the Saxon braid you can see a small heart nestled within a larger one. For a concept this pure, I chose to leave the central panel alone within the plain stockinette canvas, and it looks as if it were carved in stone, extending the image of divine permanence. The rolled stockinette edge as opposed to a traditional ribbing was to give the pullover added softness, and the organic shaping at the lower edge is a bonus design element.

The sublime pink Lamb's Pride was chosen as a close match to the overall feel of the handspun yarn. The softness of the color and the yarn lend their emotive qualities to a sweetly comfortable sweater.

The handspun yarn used has sentimental value and needed to be worked into a design this important. When I learned to spin, it soon became apparent that the amount of time spent planning a spinning project and then transforming it into a garment design gave extraordinary amounts of sentimental energy to the final knitted piece. It is sometimes a long and arduous process, fraught with trials and tribulations, including failed swatching and ripping out of knitting, but in the end, your loving work will always be there as a testament to the love and care you place upon it.

SKILL LEVEL ○ ○ ○
Experienced

FINISHED MEASUREMENTS
CHEST 38 (42, 46, 50)" (96.5 [106.5, 117, 127]cm)
LENGTH 23 (23, 25½, 25½)" (58.5 [58.5, 65, 65]cm)
Note The length from the shoulder can be varied by 2½" (6.5cm) by working more or less repeats of the pattern charts. Please allow extra yardage for additional length.

YARN medium
1,400 (1,500, 1,700, 1,800) yds
(1,280 [1,372, 1,555, 1,646]m) worsted weight
MODEL AT FRONT Handspun Blue-Faced Leicester (50%) with Mohair (50%), natural light brown
MODEL AT BACK 4, 8 (8, 9, 10) skeins Brown Sheep Company Lamb's Pride Worsted, 4 oz (113g) skeins, each approximately 190 yds (173m), 85% wool 15% mohair, M34 Victorian Pink

NEEDLES & NOTIONS
US size 5 (3.75mm) knitting needles

US size 7 (4.5mm) knitting needles, or size needed to obtain gauge
US size 5 (3.75mm) 24" (60cm) circular needle
Cable needle
Stitch marker
Tapestry needle

GAUGE
18 stitches and 26 rows = 4" (10cm) in stockinette stitch using larger needles. Adjust needle size as necessary to obtain correct gauge.

front Handspun Blue-Faced Leicester with Mohair back Brown Sheep Company Lamb's Pride Worsted

two hearts

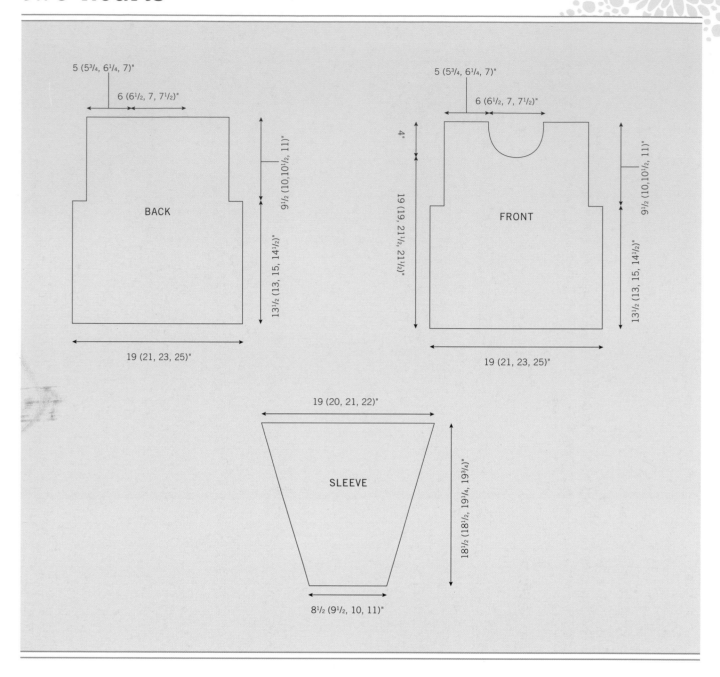

5 (5¾, 6¼, 7)"

6 (6½, 7, 7½)"

9½ (10,10½, 11)"

BACK

13½ (13, 15, 14½)"

19 (21, 23, 25)"

5 (5¾, 6¼, 7)"

6 (6½, 7, 7½)"

4"

19 (19, 21½, 21½)"

9½ (10,10½, 11)"

FRONT

13½ (13, 15, 14½)"

19 (21, 23, 25)"

19 (20, 21, 22)"

SLEEVE

18½ (18½, 19¼, 19¾)"

8½ (9½, 10, 11)"

back

With smaller needles, cast on 112 (122, 130, 140) stitches. Work in stockinette stitch for 1" (2.5cm) for rolled hem.

Main Body Pattern

SETUP ROW (RS) Change to larger needles. Work stockinette stitch over 18 (23, 27, 32) stitches, work Chart A over 13 stitches, work Chart B over center 50 stitches, work Chart A over 13 stitches, work stockinette stitch over last 18 (23, 27, 32) stitches. Continue working Charts until the piece measures 13½ (13, 15, 14½)" (34.5 [33, 38, 37]cm) from the beginning, ending with a wrong-side row.

SHAPE ARMHOLE

Bind off 7 (8, 8, 8) stitches at the beginning of the next two rows—98 (106, 114, 124) stitches. Continue until armhole measures 9½ (10, 10½, 11)" (24 [25.5, 26.5, 28]cm), ending with row 16 of Chart B. Place all stitches on holder.

front

Work as for Back until armhole measures 5½ (6, 6½, 7)" (14 [15, 16.5, 18]cm).

SHAPE NECK

Keeping continuity of Chart B, work across 38 (42, 44, 47) stitches for shoulder, place center 22 (22, 26, 30) stitches on a holder for front neck, attach a second ball of yarn, and work remaining 38 (42, 44, 47) stitches for second shoulder. Working both shoulders at the same time, decrease 1 stitch at each neck edge every other row 10 (11, 11, 11) times as follows: Work across first shoulder until 3 stitches remain, k2tog, k1 (for neck selvedge). For second shoulder, k1 (for neck selvedge), ssk, work to end—28 (31, 33, 36) stitches. Work even until Front is the same length as Back to shoulders, ending with row 16 of Chart B.

sleeves (MAKE 2)

With smaller needles, cast on 43 (47, 49, 53) stitches. Work in stockinette stitch for 1" (2.5cm), ending with a wrong-side row.

Main Sleeve Pattern

SETUP ROW (RS) Change to larger needles. Work stockinette stitch over 15 (17, 18, 20) stitches, work Chart A over center 13 stitches, work stockinette stitch over the last 15 (17, 18, 20) stitches.

SHAPE SLEEVE

Continue to work in pattern as established, increasing 1 stitch at each edge every 4 rows 15 (15, 19, 18) times, then every 6 rows 8 (8, 6, 7) times using m1 left and right accordingly—89 (93, 99, 103) stitches, working new stitches in stockinette stitch at edges. Work even until Sleeve measures 18½ (18½, 19¼, 19¾)" (47 [47, 49, 50]cm) from the beginning. Bind off all stitches.

key

☐ = K on RS, p on WS

⊡ = P on RS, k on WS

= Slip next st onto cn and hold in back, k2, p1 from cn

= Slip next 2 sts onto cn and hold in front, p1, k2 from cn

= Slip 2 sts onto cn and hold in back, k2, p2 from cn

= Slip 2 sts onto cn and hold in front, p2, k2 from cn

= Slip 2 sts onto cn and hold in back, k2, k2 from cn

= Slip 2 sts onto cn and hold in front, k2, k2 from cn

finishing

Neckband

Join the shoulders using a three-needle bind-off (page 152). With smaller circular needle and right side facing, pick up and knit 86 (92, 92, 98) stitches evenly around the neck edge, beginning at one shoulder seam, including stitches from holders. Join and mark the beginning of round. Work in stockinette stitch until the mock turtleneck measures 2–4" (5–10cm) or desired length. Bind off loosely. Sew in Sleeves and sew side seam. Weave in loose ends and block gently to measurements.

Brown Sheep Company Lamb's Pride Worsted

chart a

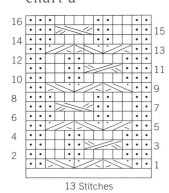

13 Stitches

chart b

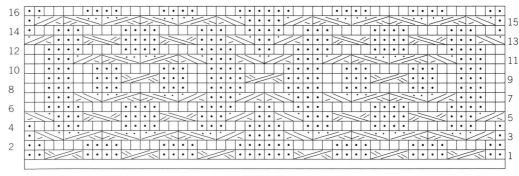

50 Stitches

GLOSSARY OF TERMS

K2TOG (KNIT TWO TOGETHER)

Insert the right needle into the first two stitches on the left needle as if to knit, knit them together as one in the usual way, dropping them off the left needle.

KITCHENER STITCH

Cut the yarn several times the length of the work and thread the yarn tail onto a tapestry needle. Holding needles parallel with wrong sides together, insert the tapestry needle as if to purl in the first stitch on the front needle. Draw the yarn through, leaving the stitch on the needle.

Insert the tapestry needle as if to knit in the first stitch on the back needle. Draw the yarn through, leaving the stitch on the needle.

*Insert the tapestry needle as if to knit in the first stitch on the front needle, and remove the stitch from the needle onto the yarn tail and draw tight.

Insert the tapestry needle as if to purl in the second stitch on the front needle, and pull through, leaving the stitch on needle.

Insert the tapestry needle as if to purl in the first stitch on the back needle, and remove the stitch from the needle onto the yarn tail and draw tight.

Insert the tapestry needle as if to knit in the second stitch of the back needle, and pull through, leaving the stitch on the needle.*

Repeat from * to * until the last stitch. Draw the yarn through the last loop and pull tight.

M1 INCREASE (MAKE ONE)

While this increase is nearly invisible, it does create a new stitch that slants in one direction or the other, depending on how it's worked. If the pattern instructions don't specify m1R or m1L, either will do.

M1L (MAKE ONE LEFT)

Insert the left needle from front to back into the horizontal bar between the last stitch worked and the next stitch. Knit or purl the bar through the back.

M1R (MAKE ONE RIGHT)

Insert the left needle from back to front into the horizontal bar between the last stitch worked and the next stitch. Knit or purl the bar through the front.

P2TOG (PURL TWO TOGETHER)

Insert the right needle into the first two stitches on the left needle as if to purl, purl them together as one in the usual way, dropping them off the left needle.

SHORT-ROW SHAPING

To wrap knit stitches: Slip the next stitch purlwise with yarn in back; bring yarn to front and slip the same stitch back onto the left needle. Turn, and bring the yarn to the front (purl side).

To wrap purl stitches: Slip the next stitch purlwise with yarn in front; move yarn to back and slip the same stitch back onto left needle. Turn, and bring the yarn to the back.

Picking up wraps on knit rows: Insert the needle under the wrap *and* the wrapped stitch knitwise, and knit them together.

Picking up wraps on purl rows: Insert the needle from behind into the back loop of the wrap and move it to left needle. Purl it together with the wrapped stitch.

SSK (SLIP, SLIP, KNIT)

Slip the next two stitches from left needle, one at a time, knitwise. Insert left needle from left to right into the front of the two slipped stitches and knit these two stitches together. Drop these two stitches as knitted off the left needle.

SSP (SLIP, SLIP, PURL)

Slip the next two stitches from left needle, one at a time, knitwise. Place these stitches back onto the left needle and insert right needle from left to right into the back of the two slipped stitches and purl these two stitches together. Drop these two stitches as purled off the left needle.

THREE-NEEDLE BIND-OFF

Place each set of stitches to be joined in the bind-off on separate needles. Matching each set of stitches and holding the pieces with right sides facing and using a third needle, k2tog one stitch from each needle and bind off in the normal manner. When joining shoulders, continue to bind off stitches of back and front shoulders, then bind off the center stitches for back neck by themselves, and use three-needle bind-off for the remaining shoulder stitches from corresponding front and back pieces.

RESOURCES

The following products and services were used in the making of the projects in this book.

Eucalan Woolwash
PO Box 374
Paris, Ontario
Canada
N3L 3T5
800-561-9731
www.eucalan.com

DRUM CARDERS
Duncan Fiber Enterprises
21740 SE Edward Drive
Clackamas, OR 97015
503-658-4066

FIBER PROCESSING
Stonehedge Fiber Mill
2246 Pesek Rd
East Jordan, MI 49727
231-536-2779
www.stonehedgefibermill.com

DYES
W. Cushing & Company
21 North Street
PO Box 351
Kennebunkport, ME 04046
800-626-7847
www.wcushing.com
Prochemical & Dye
PO Box 14
Somerset, MA 02726
800-228-9393
www.prochemical.com

ANGELINA FIBER
Textura Trading
Eastworks Building
116 Pleasant Street, Suite 343
Easthampton, MA 01027
877-839-8872
www.texturatrading.com

SPINNING RESOURCES

Refer to the following resources, books, magazines, and websites for more information about the world of spinning.

Purchasing Fiber

SPINNING FIBER AND LUXURY YARNS
Foxfire Fiber and Design
135 Reynolds Road
Shelburne, MA 01370
413-625-6121
www.foxfirefiber.com

RARE BREED YARNS AND SPINNING FIBER
Spirit Trail Fiberworks
PO Box 197
Sperryville, VA
22740-0197
www.spirit-trail.net

Books

The Ashford Book of Spinning, Anne Field (Shoal Bay Press, 1999)

Color in Spinning, Deb Menz (Interweave Press, 2005)

The Essentials of Handspinning, Mabel Ross (Mabel Ross, 1987)

Handspinning, Dyeing, and Working with Merino and Superfine Wools, Margaret Stove (Interweave Press, 2001)

Handspun Treasures from Rare Wools, Deborah Robson (Interweave Press, 2002)

In Sheep's Clothing: A Handspinner's Guide to Wool, Nola Fournier (Interweave Press, 2003)

Morehouse Farm Merino Knits, Margrit Lohrer (Potter Craft, 2006)

The Natural Knitter, Barbara Albright (Potter Craft, 2007)

Projects for Alpaca and Llama, Chris Switzer (Estes Print Works, 2004)

Spin It, Lee Raven (Interweave Press, 2003)

The Spinner's Companion, Bobbie Irwin (Interweave Press, 2001)

Spinning Designer Yarns, Diane Varney (Interweave Press, 2003)

Spinning Llama and Alpaca, Chris Switzer (Switzer Land Enterprises, 1994)

Spin to Knit, Shannon Okey (Interweave Press, 2003)

Spinning Wool: Beyond the Basics, Anne Field (Shoal Bay Press, 1995)

Magazines

SPIN-OFF, INTERWEAVE PRESS
www.interweave.com

WILD FIBERS MAGAZINE
www.wildfibersmagazine.com

Websites

NEW YORK STATE SHEEP AND WOOL FESTIVAL
www.sheepandwool.com

MARYLAND SHEEP AND WOOL FESTIVAL
www.sheepandwool.org

OKLAHOMA STATE UNIVERSITY, FOR SPECIFIC INFORMATION ON BREEDS OF SHEEP
www.ansi.okstate.edu/breeds/sheep/

THE AMERICAN LIVESTOCK BREEDS CONSERVANCY
www.albc-usa.org/

DIRECOTRY OF SHEEP BREED ASSOCIATIONS
www.nebraskasheep.com/directory/Breeds/

YARNS USED IN THIS BOOK

The following yarns are available in a wide variety of locations. Please contact the company for specific yarns. The weight and yardage per ball, as well as the CYCA ball band information (opposite) are included so accurate substitutions can be made.

Berroco Ultra Alpaca [4]

3½ oz (100g) skeins, each approximately 215 yds (198m), 50% superfine alpaca, 50% wool

BERROCO, INC.
14 Elmdale Road
Uxbridge, MA 01569
508-278-2527
www.berroco.com

Black Water Abbey Yarns Worsted Weight [4]

4 oz (114 g) skeins, each approximately 220 yds (201m), 100% wool

BLACK WATER ABBEY YARNS
PO Box 470688
Aurora, CO 80047-0688
720-320-1003
www.abbeyyarns.com

Brown Sheep Company Lamb's Pride Worsted [4]

4 oz (113g) skeins, each approximately 190 yds (173m), 85% wool 15% mohair

BROWN SHEEP COMPANY
100662 County Road 16
Mitchell, NE 69357
800-826-9136
www.brownsheep.com

Cascade 220 Wool [4]

3½ oz (100g) skeins, each approximately 220 yds (201m), 100% Peruvian Highland wool

CASCADE YARNS
1224 Andover Park E.
Tikwala, WA 98188
206-574-0440
www.cascadeyarns.com

Classic Elite Yarns Montera [4]

3½ oz (100g) skeins, each approximately 127 yds (116m), 50% llama, 50% wool

CLASSIC ELITE YARNS
122 Western Avenue
Lowell, MA 01851
978-453-2837
www.classiceliteyarns.com

Frog Tree Yarns Alpaca Sport [1]

1¾ oz (50g) skeins, each approximately 130 yds (119m), 100% alpaca

Frog Tree Alpaca Fingering [1]

1¾ oz (50g) skeins, each approximately 215 yds (197m), 100% alpaca)

FROG TREE ALPACA
PO Box 1119
East Dennis, MA 02641
508-385-8862
www.frogtreeyarns.com

Green Mountain Spinnery Maine Organic [4]

4 oz (113.5g) skeins, each approximately 250 yds (229m), 100% certified Maine organic wool

Green Mountain Spinnery Mountain Mohair [4]

2 oz (57g) skeins, each approximately 140 yds (128m), 30% mohair, 70% wool

GREEN MOUNTAIN SPINNERY
PO Box 568
Putney, VT 05346
800-321-9665
www.spinnery.com

Harrisville Designs Orchid with Cashmere [4]

3½ oz (100g) skeins, each approximately 240 yds (220m), 25% mohair, 70% fine virgin wool, 5% cashmere

HARRISVILLE DESIGNS
Center Village
PO Box 806
Harrisville, NH 03450
800-338-9415
www.harrisville.com

Jaggerspun Zephyr 2/18 Wool-Silk [1]

1 lb cone (.45k), each approximately 5,040 yds (4609m), 50% merino wool, 50% Chinese Tussah silk

JAGGERSPUN YARNS
Box 188
Springvale, ME 04083
207-324-5622
www.jaggeryarn.com

Lorna's Laces Helen's Lace [1]

4 oz (114g) skeins, each approximately 1,250 yds (1143m), 50% silk, 50% wool

Lorna's Laces Heaven [1]

7 oz (199g) skeins, each approximately 975 yds (891m), 90% kid mohair, 10% nylon

Lorna's Laces Yarns Shepherd Sock [1]

2 oz (57g) skeins, each approximately 215 yds (197m), 80% superwash wool, 20% nylon

Lorna's Laces Yarns Shepherd Sport [2]

2½ oz (74g) skeins, each approximately 200 yds (183m), 100% superwash wool

Lorna's Laces Yarns Shepherd Worsted [3]

4 oz (113.5g) skeins, each approximately 225 yds (206m), 100% superwash wool

LORNA'S LACES
4229 North Honore Street
Chicago, IL 60613
773-935-3803
www.lornaslaces.net

Reynolds Lite Lopi 4

1¾ oz (50g) skeins, each approximately 105 yds (96m), 100% Icelandic wool

REYNOLDS YARNS

JCA Crafts, Inc.
35 Scales Lane
Townsend, MA 01469
978-597-8794
www.jcacrafts.com

Rowan Felted Tweed 3

1¾ oz (50g) skeins, each approximately 192 yds (175m), 50% merino, 25% alpaca, 25% viscose/rayon

Jaeger Extra Fine Merino DK 3

1¾ oz (50g) skeins, each approximately 137 yds (125m), 100% extra fine merino DK wool

Nashua Creative Focus Worsted 5

3½ oz (100g) skeins, each approximately 220 yds (201m), 75% wool, 25% alpaca

Rowan Yarns Scottish Tweed Aran 4

3½ oz (100g) skeins, each approximately 186 yds (170m), 100% pure new wool

Rowan Yarns Scottish Tweed DK 3

1¾ oz (50g) skeins, each approximately 123 yds (113m), 100% pure new wool

WESTMINSTER FIBERS, INC.

Distributors of Rowan, Jaeger, and Nashua yarns
4 Townsend Avenue, Unit 8
Nashua, NH 03063
800-445-9276
www.westminsterfibers.com

Wooly West Footpath Yarn 1

2 oz (60g) skeins, each approximately 175 yds (160m), 85% wool, 15% nylon

THE WOOLY WEST

PO Box 58306
Salt Lake City, UT 84158
Orders (toll free) 888-487-9665
www.woolywest.com

GENERAL GUIDELINES FOR YARN WEIGHTS

The Craft Yarn Council of America has instituted a number system for knitting and crochet yarn gauges and recommended needle and hook sizes. The information provided below is intended as a guideline, and as always, swatching is key to being sure a chosen yarn is a good match for the intended project. More information can be found at www.yarnstandards.com.

CYCA	1	2	3	4	5
Yarn Weight	**SUPER FINE** Lace, Fingering, Sock	**FINE** Sport	**LIGHT** DK, Light Worsted	**MEDIUM** Worsted, Aran	**BULKY** Chunky
Avg. Knitted Gauge over 4" (10cm)	27–32 sts	23–26 sts	21–24 sts	16–20 sts	12–15 sts
Recommended Needle in US Size Range	1–3	3–5	5–7	7–9	9–11
Recommended Needle in Metric Size Range	2.25–3.25mm	3.25–3.75mm	3.75–4.5mm	4.5–5.5mm	5.5–8mm

Ackowledgments and thank-yous worthy of an Oscar speech

A book with this many finished pieces couldn't be done without test knitters. Heartfelt thanks to all of you and your wonderful knitting: Teresa Campbell, Alexandra Garven, Mary Beth Irwin, Lauren Lax, Jordana Paige, Suzanne Reyes, Darlene Willard, Annie Will.

Thanks to the companies who provided yarn for this book and thanks to the sheep, goats, alpacas, llamas, and their shepherds who provided their fiber for the handspun garments in this book.

Thanks to my agent, Linda Roghaar. Thanks to Rosy Ngo, Erin Slonaker, Amy Sly, and the staff at Potter Craft. Thanks to Peggy Greig and her technical editing and wonderful graphics.

With special thanks to Bruce Hornsby and Don Henley for writing "The End of the Innocence," which inspired Halcyon after September 2001. A few stitches as my attempt to mend the hole in the world.

Soundtrack provided by Bruce Hornsby: www.brucehornsby.com

Photo opposite: Handspun Romney/Border Leicester crossbred and Mohair, for the St. Patrick sweater, page 108.

Index